MY FIGHT TO THE TOP

Michelle Mone

MY FIGHT TO THE TOP

Michelle Mone

WITH RUTH KELLY

BLINK
bringing you closer

Published by Blink Publishing
3.25, The Plaza,
535 Kings Road,
Chelsea,
London, SW10 0SZ

www.blinkpublishing.co.uk

facebook.com/blinkpublishing
twitter.com/blinkpublishing

PB – 978-1-910536-66-7

A CIP catalogue of this book is available from the British Library.

Design by www.envydesign.co.uk

Printed and bound by Clays Ltd, St Ives Plc

1 3 5 7 9 10 8 6 4 2

Papers used by Blink Publishing are natural, recyclable products made from
wood grown in sustainable forests. The manufacturing processes conform to the
environmental regulations of the country of origin.

Blink Publishing is an imprint of the Bonnier Publishing Group
www.bonnierpublishing.co.uk

CONTENTS

PREFACE

Maybe it was all that bullying and heartache that drove me to success.

My childhood was dominated by struggle and tragedy. I slept in the bedroom cupboard in my parents' bedroom in Glasgow's rough East End; I was bullied, rushed to hospital after being beaten by a gang of ten and cried myself to sleep every night after my father became paralysed from the waist down.

I became a young mum at 20 and almost lost my second child when he was born four weeks premature. The pressure of trying to build a business and be a good mother brought my marriage, and my health, to the edge. At my lowest point, I ballooned to size 22 and contemplated suicide.

I swung from the extremes of being on the brink of bankruptcy, to having millions in the bank. I revelled in the highs of driving flash cars and dining out with some of the world's most famous icons, such as the Clintons. I almost drowned in the lows of the very public breakdown of my marriage. My name was dragged through the tabloids as it was revealed that my husband was having an affair with my chief designer. And I then had to battle to win back the business I started from scratch.

I have been on a journey, which on the face of it looks very glamorous – walking down red carpets and appearing on the pages of *Hello* magazine. But the reality has been a tough ride, blighted by pain and hardship.

That's why my story is different: my story will offer inspiration and hope – whether you'd like to learn how to get ahead in business, or simply learn how to hold yourself up through life's challenges. My pain, my life, my business: this is *My Fight to the Top*.

SHOOTING FOR THE STARS

Allow yourself to be a beginner.
No one starts off being excellent.

There is no doubt in my mind that I've got to where I am today because of where I grew up. My drive came from looking around me and wanting more.

It doesn't matter how much money I've got in the bank or how many deals I've done the day before – I still wake up every morning with the fear of failure. It feels like someone has pulled my insides into a knot and I can't breathe. I think about what my ex-husband, Michael, used to say to me:

'One day, you'll be back in the ghetto.'

To call the East End of Glasgow 'the ghetto' is awful, because the people who live there are some of the nicest you will ever meet. They are caring, they are generous and they will give you their last drop of milk even if it leaves them short. I love the people I grew up with but I just don't want the life my mum and dad had – always struggling. My biggest fear is that one day

I'll be in the same situation I was in as I was being brought up. So that's why I never give up. No matter what challenges life throws at me, I'll still pull myself out of bed the next morning, and get on with it. That's what I had to do when I was growing up and that's what I do to this day.

When I look back on my childhood I feel very grateful to my mum and dad for looking after me and always making me feel loved, especially as I know it wasn't easy for them. I was born in the Gallowgate, the heart of the East End, in 1971. It was where the working class lived. My mum and dad will swear we weren't poor because people in the East End never complained. They accepted the hand they were dealt and just got on with it.

But the truth is, we were poor. We did struggle. My mum worked two jobs to keep our heads above water – she stitched coats and dresses at the Singer sewing machine factory and worked at the fruit and veg shop over the weekend. My dad worked in a factory as well, making ink for newspaper printing. He used to get up at 5.30 am and come home long after it got dark. Never, ever, would they think of having a sick day. If either of them had the flu they would still fight their way to work. Their work ethic of 'You must work hard for your money' quickly rubbed off on me.

My first memories are of living in Dennistoun in Glasgow when I was between five and six. Our home was at 25 Bathgate Street and I remember my mum explaining we had to move there after our previous home in a block of flats was condemned due to a rat infestation. We settled in a traditional tenement building. To get to our flat you had to climb a cold, concrete stairwell that smelt of damp.

Inside, there was only one bedroom and a tiny kitchen in the lounge. Mum hung a bead curtain to separate the two areas. The ceilings were really high, something that made the rooms seem spooky when the lights were turned out. There was a cupboard off my mum and dad's bedroom and that was my room. It was so small there wasn't even enough space to fit my bed until my dad shortened it by a foot.

I was a real daddy's girl; he would do anything for me. He came home one night carrying a big block of wood and he used that to lower the ceiling. We then stuck sparkly stickers all over it so I could pretend I was gazing up at the stars – I was reaching for the stars, even back then. Mine was the tiniest room, but the best. I felt safe curled up in my den, listening to my parents breathe in the bedroom next to me.

We didn't have a bath or a shower in our tiny, wee bathroom, just a toilet. Once a week, my mum would take me to Whitevale Baths to get washed. The pools were by the high-rise flats that towered over the rest of the estate and looked like something out of a horror film. Mum warned me never to go near them or I wouldn't be coming back.

It cost ten pence to enter the red-brick Baths building and I would get my own cubicle with a big iron bath. I could see under and over the wooden doorframe and I would stay in there for as long as I could before I'd get chapped out. I'd hear a rat-a-tat-tat on the door. 'Oi, hurry up, next person in,' I'd be told. I'd leap out onto the cold tiles, dry myself and throw my clothes back on.

We would often stop by the steamy whilst we were down there. The steamy is what you would probably now call the launderette. I'd help Mum carry the bundles of sheets and

Mum would scrub them over a big block of wood in the industrial sinks. Her fingers looked like shrivelled prunes by the end of it. I used to help my mum put the sheets through the big iron rollers to squish out the excess.

We used to have traditional East End food like mince and potatoes for supper. Nothing fancy. If we had fillet steak, it would be at Christmas. On Fridays I would go down the chippy. I'd get fish for mum and dad and I'd get myself a sausage supper, which came with chips and onion gravy. I'd run there and run back and we'd eat off our knees in front of the TV. But supper at our house was gourmet compared to what my granny used to serve up. I used to go to Granny Allan's house in the school holidays because my mum and dad were working full-time and couldn't look after me. My granny, my dad's mum, was a tough woman, Glaswegian through and through. She lived in the really rough part of the East End, in Haghill.

Granny made me eat chicken liver and onions, or tripe. She used to boil tripe in milk. Oh, my god! 'Please, Granny, don't make me eat that,' I'd whimper.

'Do you know how much that cost?' Granny would shove it back it under my nose. 'You eat to survive.' Even now, when I go to Michelin-starred restaurants and see liver on the menu, I almost want to puke. I used to sneak to Coia's Cafe on Duke Street for an ice cream. You would have to bring your own glass bowl and they would fill it up with a couple of scoops.

My dad's escape was to go to the pub on the corner. It was called the Dog and Rabbit but all the locals called it the Dug. Mum would send me there on my bike to get him to come home for dinner. 'I'm about to put his bloody dinner in the bin,' she'd yell, so I'd get on my bike and peddle to the Dug as fast as I could. I'd stand on my tiptoes and try and beckon him through the window. If that didn't work, I'd snake my way through the doors and plead with him to come home.

'Please, Dad, don't spend all the wages,' I'd beg. I didn't like it when he drank a lot because he would fight with Mum. Mum could shout really loudly and I would sometimes hold my hands over my ears. But that's the way it was for most couples. That was the East End life – you worked hard and you went to the bingo or the bookies to see if you could get that extra bit of cash. It would always be, 'Oh, my god, Jimmie won on the horses,' or 'Oh, my god, Isabel won at the bingo,' and then everyone would go around their house to get a free drink and celebrate.

We didn't have much, but what we did have, was a community. You never used to lock your door. If you wanted something, you would go and bang on someone's door. 'Shops are shut. Can I have some of your sugar?' And they would give you their last bit of sugar, even if it would leave them short. If you knocked on the door of an apartment in Mayfair in London they would phone the police!

This sense of community meant it was also a very happy time, because some of the best parties could be found in the East End. They would be at my aunties', my uncle's and at my flat. Probably after someone had won on the horses or at the bingo. I remember one party in our flat because they were playing Rod Stewart music loud enough for the whole of the estate to hear. I shouted up at my mum from our backyard.

'Mum, I'm starving, can you throw me a piece of bread and jam?'

She popped her head out the window, disappeared and a few

minutes later a jam sandwich, wrapped in foil, came hurtling down. I gobbled it up and then carried on playing with my friends from the neighbourhood. I was dancing around, pretending to be like the grown-ups. I was very tall and skinny for my age with long, dark-blonde hair. When everyone had left I sat on my mum's knee and cuddled into her. Her warmth would spread over me like a blanket.

That was one of my last happy memories.

I was seven when Dad started limping. Family and friends used to think he was drunk but I knew immediately that something was seriously wrong. The doctors thought Dad had cancer and he had to go back and forth to the hospital to have tumours removed. Every time Dad came home his limp was worse and he looked in even more pain. He tried to hide his suffering from me, but the agony was etched into his face. Mum would cry all the time and I would listen to her sobbing from my little bedroom. I felt utterly helpless. Every night I would hug my pillow and quietly cry myself to sleep, thinking my dad wouldn't be alive in the morning. Some nights I would lie awake for hours, craning my ear against the door to listen out for my dad's breathing.

It was one thing after another from then on. I can't remember us having a normal Christmas after that. It was always spent around my dad's hospital bed at the Royal or in the Chinese restaurant across the road from his ward. I can't even remember my mum being pregnant. It must have been while Dad was having all his operations. All I can see when I look back is my mum, lying on the couch, heavily pregnant and then the next thing I know, she is rushed away in an ambulance. I went with my Aunty Margaret to the hospital but my family wouldn't let me see my mum. I started screaming and crying and my aunty had to hold me down.

'I want to see the baby, I want to see my brother,' I cried.

But my family had formed a wall and I wasn't getting through. 'Calm down, Michelle, you're not seeing him.' Aunty Margaret sat me down.

'I want my mum, I want my mum,' I sobbed. I screamed and cried for my mum and brother for several days. My throat felt like sandpaper and I could barely speak. When my mum finally came home, she didn't have my brother with her. Her eyes were bloodshot from her tears and her face was as white as ash. My mum was too sad to speak to me. She just wanted to lie on the couch and watch television. Sometimes I wasn't even sure if she was watching the screen or just staring into space. I was met with a wall of silence from the rest of my family. No explanations – nobody told me anything. It was how things were back then; you just got on with it. I knew in my heart my baby brother hadn't made it, but it wasn't until years later that I found out he had died from spina bifida.

I don't remember the funeral and I can't seem to remember anything else about the death of my brother. Perhaps because there was so much going on at the time, too much heartache, I just blanked it all out. I think that's why my dad went to the pub all the time – because there were too many tears and fights going on at home. There was drama all the time. I was always on tenterhooks, always on the watch for what was coming up around the corner.

You had to grow eyes in the back of your head if you wanted to survive in my neighbourhood. I learnt this the hard way when I was eight years old. Something happened to me I can never forget. I was playing on my roller skates in the next street with my friend. She needed to get something from her flat on the top floor.

'Hang on a minute,' I called after her, as I still had my skates on.

I started climbing the concrete staircase in my boots, carefully side-stepping so as not to roll backwards. Suddenly, out of nowhere, I felt a big hand clamp around my ankle like a vice. I spun around to see a man with a creepy smile across his face. I screamed and I tried to run up the stairs, but I couldn't. I kept falling down because of my roller skates. The man grabbed my leg and tried to pull me into his flat. I was screaming and wriggling as he dragged me down the stairs.

'Leave me alone, leave me alone,' I screamed. My nails were scratching across the concrete as he dragged me. Suddenly, I found my strength and I kicked him in the face with my roller skate. He fell crashing back and I got away. I don't know how I managed to run up those flight of stairs so quickly.

I was hysterical as I came crashing through my friend's door. My whole body was shaking with terror. If he had taken me into his flat, I think I would have been raped. I could barely get my words out so my friend's dad explained the attack to my mum and dad. My mum flew around there. My dad was too poorly to climb down the stairs, which was probably a good thing, as god knows what he would have done to the guy. I never knew what happened to him, apart from that it had been taken care of. Mum said she went around there and 'gave him a warning'.

I was terrified of going to go to see my friend after that. I waited for her on the street outside. I never had a peaceful night's sleep after the attack. I always felt fearful. I became like a dog, always on the lookout. I became so streetwise – I learnt to read body language, I could tell when someone was about to attack and I learnt how to suss out situations within seconds. I knew where to go and where not to go. Some areas I knew never to go near, like the high-rises by the steamy. You had to know, to survive in the East End. Without a doubt, my intuition is the reason I'm a success in business. I know how to deal with anyone in front of me. I know how to negotiate with them. I would not be the person I am today if I hadn't learnt those life lessons growing up.

It was my other gran, my mum's mum, who first noticed there was something different about me. 'I'm telling you, that Michelle, she's going to be someone some day,' she'd tell my mum.

Gran Philips was the posh gran. She was from Dumbarton. She used to iron her banknotes and that's where I get my attitude to money. Whenever I get cash out, I have to put them in numerical order before I can do anything else. All my notes are crisp and organised.

Gran had a heart of gold. She would put everyone else before herself. She used to fold up £10 notes and slip them into the palm of anyone she thought needed it more than herself. And not just money either: whenever she heard a baby was born she gave a blanket. Even if she didn't know the family, she would crochet a little hat. She was such a kind, incredible woman – she was like Mother Teresa and everyone knew of her.

My gran was a nurse for many years. Her husband left her when my mum was a wee girl and Gran never met anyone after that. She was a single mum bringing up three kids and working constantly – night shifts at the hospital. I think that was why she became an alcoholic. But Gran nearly burnt the house down when my mum was little and she never touched a drop after that. She joined Alcoholics Anonymous and even though she was sober for 45 years she would always tell you she was an alcoholic. She wouldn't even touch the trifle at Christmas time because she warned us that 'the taste of it will send you straight back'.

Back when I was growing up, my gran would get the train into town once a week on a Saturday and we would all go for a Chinese or a high tea together. I remember going to a restaurant with her and my mum when I was seven and scowling at the paper table cover. There were food stains all over it. 'I'm not eating off that,' I said. My mum and gran stared at me in disbelief. It wasn't like I was spoilt; I just wasn't prepared to eat off a dirty table. I had standards that I would not compromise on.

'Michelle is going to be something one day. Her attention to detail is something else.' Gran Philips smiled.

'Stop it, Mum,' my mum shrugged.

'No, Isabel, Michelle knows exactly what she wants, she's going to go far in life, mark my words.' My gran knew. She was like a white witch. She used to read everyone's tea leaves and she must have seen the future in mine.

I wasn't like everyone else my age. For starters, I didn't have the usual pin-ups that my other friends had, like Madonna and Spandau Ballet. No, above my bed was a picture of Richard Branson. I wanted to be him – a success. I would watch *Dallas* and *Dynasty* with my sausage supper on my knees and I thought, One day, I'll have that sports car. One day, I'll have that big house with the sweeping staircase. One day, I'll be able to look after my mum and dad.

So when I was ten, I decided I wanted to earn money. I persuaded the newspaper shop on our street that I could deliver the papers. There were a lot of them but I was determined – I started off my rounds in the evening after school, then I did the Sunday papers, and then I delivered the *Daily Record* in the mornings. It was too much for one girl to take on by herself so I decided to hire a load of other kids. Pretty soon I had 17 teenagers working for me. I'd give them the streets and I'd take a cut of their earnings. Can you imagine, a wee ten-year-old bossing around all these teenagers? My gran was right, I was different!

Of course, it wasn't too long before some of the kids wanted more money. A few of the boys asked to meet with me up the back of the Dyke, the name of a wall in the East End. The boys were standing on the wall, looking down at me.

'We are three years older than you. We are going to take your paper round off you,' one of them started to say. I can't tell you how angry I felt. Just because I was a girl, just because I was younger than them, how dare they? No way were they going to bully me. I folded my arms across my chest.

'Don't you even think about coming on my patch,' I blasted. 'I started the paper round. If you want to start your own paper round and not work for me any more, fine, but you're not taking over the East End, this is mine.' The boys started getting aggressive, but I was having none of it. 'I'm not going to even argue with you. This is business. And I'll push you off that dyke right now.' I couldn't help myself.

Their jaws just dropped. They'd never seen anything like it. I walked off feeling victorious.

My first of many victories.

2

PASSION AND DETERMINATION

*I am who I am today because of the
choices I made yesterday.*

'Where do you think you're going?' one of the girls from my school shouted as she pushed me in the back. I'd had enough of her bullying. I swung around and pushed her away.

'Stop it right now,' I warned her. The next thing I knew, ten teenagers from the same gang appeared out of nowhere. They formed a ring around us and started chanting.

'Fight! Fight!'

We looked at each other but neither of us really wanted to fight. The boys had worked themselves up in a frenzy, though, and wanted to see us tear pieces out of each other. I edged away but they pushed me back into the ring.

One of the boys went for me, kicking me to the ground.

Smack.

Another boy joined in. The pain exploded in my body.

Smack, smack, smack.

I didn't stand a chance against all of them. They kicked and punched me until I was left unconscious. The next thing I remember was waking up in hospital with my mum and dad beside my bed. I was in so much pain I couldn't move. My face and my whole body were black and blue. There was a man from the Criminal Investigation Department (CID) standing at the end of my bed, asking my mum questions. Mum explained to the officer how she had found me.

'I went up Duke Street to pick Michelle up from Thompson Street primary,' Mum started to tell the officer. Through my swollen eyelids I watched him take notes. 'But she wasn't there, so I came back along Bathgate Street and all the kids came running up to me shouting Michelle's name. I couldn't make sense of what they were saying.'

'What's happened? I said.'

"Michelle is lying on the stairs. She's been beaten up," the kids told me.

'My heart stopped. I found Michelle lying there. Her whole body was red because the bruises hadn't even come out yet. I called an ambulance and went with her to The Royal.'

I couldn't remember anything of what my mum had just told the man. I started to cry but the tears burnt my cheeks.

'Michelle, are you okay to tell us what happened?' The CID officer turned to face me.

'Uh-huh,' I said, wiping my eyes with my bruised hands.

I told him everything I remembered before I had passed out.

This wasn't the first time I had been bullied. The school I went to was really tough – kids had already threatened to beat me up. It had got to the stage where I was petrified to go to class. I think it was because I wasn't like the other kids, so I got it in the neck for being 'different'. One day, I woke up, and realised that if I didn't stand up to them, my life would become an utter misery. That's why I pushed the girl back when she went for me. *That's what you've got to do with bullies, stand up to them or they will keep on bullying you.*

'Do you want us to press charges? That's not just a hit, they were kicking your wee girl,' the CID officer asked my mum and dad.

'No, I just want to give them a serious warning, make sure they don't ever do it again,' my mum decided. My injuries were so bad I was in hospital for three days before I was finally allowed home.

By now we had moved into a ground-floor flat across the street from our old flat because Dad was too poorly to walk up and down the stairs. We'd moved nearby because that was what happened in the East End: if you moved, it would be to the next street or the same street but across the road. I finally had my own bedroom with a side table, an addition which meant a lot to me.

My mum and dad were really worried about my injuries and mum kept popping her head around the door to check if I needed anything. But I've never been one to sit around and mope. I came from a place where you learn to shut up and get on with it. I know it sounds like a cliché, but what doesn't kill you makes you stronger. With every knock, with every beating, I felt stronger. I went back to school with my head held high because I'd stood up to those bullies and the 'serious warning' helped because they left me alone for a while. I was soon at Whitehill secondary school where I was focused on finding another job, earning more money.

This is what I had: passion, determination and a 'can-do' attitude. If you've got those ingredients, nothing will stop you.

My mum had worked for George the Fruitie at the weekends so when I was 12, I decided to ask him for a job. His shop was on the high street – Duke Street – not far from our flat. I can't remember how much he hired me for but it wouldn't have been much back in those days. My job was to pack all the potatoes, weigh all the fruits and help George with his 'marketing' and 'customer services'.

As soon as the school bell went at 3.45 pm I'd run down to his shop, ready to start working at 4 pm. My friends would ask where I was going, wanting me to stay on and hang out with them, but I had work to do. Nothing was coming between me and work. I worked a full day on Saturday as well.

The fruit shop wars were going on in the East End, so I wanted to do everything in my power to make George Number one. I used to slice up a few strawberries from new deliveries and hand them out as samples. 'You really need to taste these,' I smiled, holding out a sliver to try. On the Saturday morning I spent most of my time outside, fixing the display. I built all the boxes up and tilted them onto their side. It was the best show of fruit you could imagine.

I must have done a good job, because a year later, I was headhunted by the sweet shop across the road – Pick A Pack. I was offered ten pence more an hour. I had to tell George I was leaving him. 'Good luck, darling,' he said. George was a lovely man.

I'll never forget getting my first pay packet from Pick A Pack. I got a bus into town, went into something like an Argos and I spent my savings on new kitchen gear for my mum. I bought her a bin, a kitchen-roll holder, a toilet-roll holder and a toilet brush. My wee arms felt like they were going to tear out of their sockets as I carried the goods home. But no effort was too big to help my parents.

Equally, Mum and Dad would spend their last penny on me if they could. Mum would pay for me to enter dancing competitions and beauty shows to boost my confidence. They scrimped and saved to send me to elocution lessons because they wanted to better my chances in life. I'll always be grateful to them for that. Elocution lessons seemed to me to be like a finishing school because I already had good manners. Mum and Dad had always taught me to be polite, but I did speak like an East End girl – that's where I was from after all. The teacher would make me practise asking for my groceries.

'I would like a pint of milk, please,' I'd repeat after her. It was very different to what I was used to. People in the East End would say, 'Gimme a pint of milk'.

Mum would always make sure I had a good outfit to wear to my Saturday lessons. She used to stitch clothes such as dresses and pinafores. Perhaps that's where my passion for design first came from. She had a sewing machine and if she saw fabric lying around, she would turn it into a new creation.

I was grateful to my parents for helping me but the elocution lessons and the clothes did leave me open to attack. 'Posh girl', they used to call me at school. 'She thinks she's something special,' they'd whisper behind my back. It also didn't help that I was one of the few girls who actually wore the school uniform. Most of the kids would turn up in tracksuits and trainers but my parents insisted I looked smart.

'Please, Mum, don't make me wear this.' I'd beg her to let me be like the other kids.

'No, you're wearing it, and that's the end of it,' Mum cut me dead. She was right to insist; you should always look well turned out. Back then I was just terrified of being beaten up again.

Mum's words rubbed off on me, though, because I made sure I always looked impeccable for my next job. I was 13 when I forged my mum's signature so I could be an Avon rep. You had to be 18 to do that kind of door-to-door sales but I couldn't wait until then: I wanted to make more money. I might have been shy around my friends but when it came to work, I had this armour of confidence that I would throw on. I could sell anything; I could sell sand to the Arabs. I used to go home, change into my smart clothes (I had a perm at the time too) and then I'd go from door to door. I'd collate orders, put them through the area manager and then collect all the money.

Customers probably thought, Who's this nice wee girl on my doorstep? But then I would deliver the most aggressive sales pitch ever. I'd go through each sales product, giving them the features and the benefits, and tell them how amazing they were going to look. 'If you buy that,' I'd say, pointing to some lotion, 'then you really need to have the set.' I'd always push. 'It's no good having something that you don't have the whole set of because you're not getting the full benefit of those products.'

I always made a sale. And if I couldn't at first, I kept on at that person until I had. 'I'm not interested in buying on the door,' they might say. But I kept going back and back again until I'd made a sale. Within six months I was the best selling Avon rep in Glasgow. I'm not kidding – and the best bit was they didn't have a clue how old I really was. They thought I was my mum! My mum knew I was selling, because all the stuff would be delivered to our tiny flat, but she didn't know it was in her name.

Mum had enough on her plate to worry about anyway. My dad was now struggling to walk, even with a stick. He had to give up his job at the printers and there was a lot of pressure on my mum to look after Dad and still earn a living. Mum used to cry and shout and I felt helpless because I didn't know how to make things better. I didn't want to burden my mum with my heartache, so I would go to my room after dinner, and quietly cry into my pillow. I would never stay the night around friends' houses because I couldn't bring myself to leave my dad's side. What if something happened? What if I couldn't be there to help him? I would never forgive myself.

I think feeling completely and utterly helpless manifested itself as OCD – obsessive compulsive disorder. I wanted to help my mum so I would repeatedly clean our tiny kitchen. I'd scrub the surfaces until they sparkled and then I'd do it all over again. I had to make sure all the labels on the tins faced the same way. I believed everything should have its own place – something that has stuck with me through until now. I'm not sure why I did it. Maybe because everything else in my life was out of control it was my way of creating some order.

It was hard for me to focus at school while there was so much heartache going on at home. It didn't help that I was dyslexic and struggled so much with my reading and writing. I dreaded going into class because I found it so hard and none of the teachers were really interested. I did have a small group of friends who I'd hang around with. They were from the posh end of the East End, the Parade, where people owned their own houses. Even with these friends I'd never let on what was going on at home. I was afraid if I did, I wouldn't be able to stop myself crying.

I didn't think things could get any worse but the worst blow was to come. I had come home from school on what had been a normal day but as soon as I opened the front door I knew something was seriously wrong. My mum's face looked the colour of stone. Her eyes were bloodshot. The atmosphere in the room was as if someone had died.

'What's wrong?' I said. I could feel the pain before I saw it.

My mum didn't need to say a word. There was my dad – in a wheelchair. I clasped my mouth with my hand.

'Dad?' I cried.

'Your dad's not going to be able to walk again,' Mum broke the news.

I burst into tears. I couldn't take any more. I loved my dad and I thought this was the end. 'It's going to be okay, Michelle,' Dad tried to reassure me but I could tell by his eyes he didn't believe what he was telling me.

'What's happened?' I sobbed. I was 15 but I suddenly felt like a wee girl again – small and helpless.

'Your dad's got hemangioma,' my mum said. 'It's a rare condition that attacks the spinal chord.' Her voice started to tremble.

'I'll explain to her, Isabel,' my dad interrupted. 'It's when blood vessels in the spine get bigger and bigger and trap the nerves.' It didn't matter how they explained it, the truth was my dad had become completely and utterly paralysed at the age of 38. There was so much sadness in that room, I can't even begin to describe it.

I lost all interest in school after that. All I could think about was helping my mum and dad. The final straw came in a meeting with my career guidance teacher. 'So, Michelle, what do you want to do when you leave school?' she asked.

'I want to be an entrepreneur,' I announced. That's what Richard Branson was and that's what I too was going to be.

She looked utterly puzzled by what I had just said. 'What's that?' she scowled.

I had to explain to my own teacher what it meant. She told me that she very much doubted that's what I would become because I wasn't very academic. She said I wasn't great at school. 'There's a Co-op supermarket being built at the end of Duke Street. Maybe you should go and apply for a job there?'

There wasn't anything wrong with being on the checkout, but I thought, No, I can do better than this. I also thought, Why am I here? What exactly are you giving me? If my teachers didn't take any interest in me, then why the bloody hell should I bother? Sod you, I'm off! I left school at 15 with no qualifications. I had the school board chasing me for a while but I didn't care. I'd broken the cycle of what normally happens to girls in the East End.

I wasn't academic, but I was determined, and I was already on my path to success.

3

BE YOURSELF

*I'd rather be disliked for who I am
than liked for who I'm not.*

I guess it would be fair to say I was as ambitious in love as in my work. It would have been very easy for me to end up with an East End guy, but I didn't want that. I knew that if I did, then I would never get out. A few of the girls in my class had got pregnant at 14. That's what life was like – you got pregnant, you got a house from the council and you never get out of the East End. Don't get me wrong, I didn't think there was anything wrong with that, it just wasn't me. I had ambition. My drive came from looking around me and wanting more.

I'd been on a few dates after I finished school, but they were nothing serious. I wasn't ready for having a boyfriend; I was too busy thinking about making a career for myself. So I decided to put to good use the modelling classes my mum and dad had sent me to. I was starting to look quite glamorous by the time I was 16. I was tall, thin and I'd got rid of the perm. I always made an effort to blow-dry my long, blonde hair straight and I would wear eye make-up and lip gloss. I passed as older than I was, which helped me get my first modelling job – as a Tennent's girl.

Tennent's was the famous East End brewery, so you can imagine how proud my mum and dad were to have their daughter on the face of every lager can. My dad would have been down the pub showing off to all his friends. I got a real buzz from seeing myself every time I went into the shops. I felt it was a sign of my future to come. I was no longer just another face in the crowd. No, I stood out.

Unfortunately, it didn't last very long as Tennent's found out I was only 16 and sacked me. You couldn't have an underage girl as the face of an alcohol brand! It didn't stop me modelling. I'd made a bit of a name for myself and I was constantly being booked for promo work. Looking back, it was a happy time, because my work brought my family closer together. My mum and dad would get excited about seeing my face in the local paper and my dad drove me all over Scotland in our new disabled car so I'd be at my job on time. Those moments we shared in the car, chatting away, meant a lot to me. I'd always been a daddy's girl and it reminded me of the happy times we had before Dad had got ill.

The disabled car was one of several things that we now had to make my mum and dad's life easier. We'd also got a bungalow from the council, which was next to the Barras. The Barras is a very famous Glasgow market where you could pick up all sorts of cheap goods – that's where you went for your three-towels-for-a-fiver. The area was also known for being rough as hell and was often in the news for murders and all sorts, but we thought we had won the lottery. It was our first house with our own front door.

The more modelling work I got, the more confident I grew and the more ambitious I became. I was getting lots of attention from guys but I hadn't yet met anyone who shared the same goals as me. So I didn't take much notice when Michael first started chatting me up at a money show in the SECC (the Scottish Exhibition and Conference Centre). He was a financial advisor and I was a hostess on his stall. Yes, I was instantly attracted to him, he was a good-looking guy, but I thought he was married.

'Do you want to go out for a drink?' he asked.

Was he joking? I gave him a filthy look. 'No, you're wearing a wedding band.'

For a split second he looked confused. 'Honestly, I'm not married,' he laughed. 'My mum got me this ring as a present but I've got dermatitis on this hand.' Michael waved his right hand. 'That's why I wear it on my ring finger.'

'Bollocks,' I laughed. I don't suffer fools gladly.

Michael brought his dad to the show the next day to prove to me he was telling the truth. His dad was a gentleman, a consultant anaesthetist. With a well-spoken voice, he confirmed Michael's story about why he wore the ring on his wedding finger. I was impressed that Michael had gone to such lengths to win me over, so I thought, Okay, why not? I'll go on a date with you. I was 17 and impressionable and he was five years older. We became close very quickly – there was chemistry and Michael was so charming. I guess you could say I was swept off my feet. Michael joked about marrying me a couple of weeks after we first started going out.

We couldn't have had more different backgrounds – I was working class, he was middle class. Michael had grown up in Newlands, which is very posh. He'd gone to private school. His mum and dad both had very professional jobs – his mum was also a consulting doctor. But what I liked most about Michael was that he also had a professional job. None of the guys I knew from the East End had professional jobs. It was a turn-on because it wasn't what I was used to. And I suppose I was a turn-on for him because I was different. I was a young, good-looking girl from the rough side of town. He also liked me because I had plans. I was always coming up with my own business ideas, even back then. We would stay up for hours chatting about how we were going to get rich.

My mum and dad were nervous for me because Michael was so different. 'God, he lives in Newlands. God, his mum and dad are doctors. We are working class, we live in the East End,' they used to say. I think they were worried that Michael would eventually go back to 'his own kind' and end up marrying a girl from his background. They didn't want to see their wee girl's heart broken.

'Don't worry, Mum and Dad, I can handle myself,' I reassured them. I wasn't going to let someone's background intimidate me. Yes, it was all a bit daunting, but I had decided: I am who I am and if you don't accept me, then that is your loss. I believed that being confident with being yourself was key to being successful.

Saying that, I did spend some time choosing my outfit for my first dinner with his parents. I wanted to impress them. I didn't want them to think less of me because I came from the other side of town. I bought an outfit specially; a stripy, white-and-black jacket worn over a dress. I looked very respectable, very conservative. There was no cleavage hanging out. I looked the part. But I was so nervous visiting his home for the first time. I felt like I was going into Buckingham Palace. His parents had a grand, old house with its own driveway. It smelt clean and fresh when you walked into the hallway. The furniture and decorations in the lounge were perfectly matching and pristine. I got butterflies in my belly because I suddenly felt out of my comfort zone. I was myself though, that's all I could be.

Michael's dad was lovely, very welcoming. His mum was a bit, hmm, she's from the East End. We later became close and I think she respected me for working hard, but when she first met me, you could tell she was disappointed. I could see it in her eyes.

I was very polite. Give them their due, my mum and dad and my gran have brought me up with manners. I learnt that no matter where you are from, no matter what money you have got or, what education you managed to get, you use your manners to treat people with respect.

We sat down at the table – it was beautifully laid for dinner. I was admiring the whole set-up when, suddenly, my heart stopped. I actually didn't know which piece of bread to take – should I go for the one on the left of my plate or on the right? Don't forget, up to this point I'd only eaten dinner off my knees in front of the TV.

Oh, my god.

I didn't know whether to use the big knife and fork first or the smaller set that was positioned on their outside.

What do I do? What do I do? I panicked.

So I just smiled.

I waited for everyone else to pick up their bread.

It's to the left, it's to the left, I drilled in my head.

And then I watched everyone pick up their knives and forks – they started outside, working in.

Great, I've got that as well.

I taught myself table manners that night. I came away from dinner knowing what a red and a white wine glass was, but I also returned home feeling even more determined about what I wanted from life. I too wanted to raise a family in a big house, in the posh part of town.

Eleven months after we first met, Michael surprised me one night by turning up at my house in a brand new Mercedes. Oh, my god, can you imagine a flash car parked outside our wee bungalow? Everyone was leaning out of their windows saying, 'What the hell is going on?'

'What are you doing?' I came out of my house in my slippers.

'Come on, it's a surprise.' He grinned.

I knew there and then that something was going on. It sounds cheesy but I felt like a fairy-tale princess being swept away, being rescued by her prince. Michael had borrowed the Mercedes from his neighbours, Ben and Ilene, because he wanted to impress me. He took me for dinner at a fancy restaurant and asked me to marry him. I knew that as soon as I got married I was out of the East End. That's not why I said 'Yes' to Michael because I really loved him, but I knew Michael would never want to live where I grew up. I was 18. My mum and dad were happy for me because they could see I was in love. There was one small obstacle that stood in our way though.

I was part of the Church of Scotland (Protestant), and Michael was Catholic. Michael felt strongly about his religion and told me he wanted me to convert. It was a big thing in the

East End to be marrying a Catholic, let alone to be changing your religion. I wanted to marry Michael so I did it for him. I went to Catholic lessons three nights a week. My mum and dad have always supported my decisions but I can imagine their friends had a few words to say about it.

We started planning the wedding and got as far as setting the date, booking the band and choosing the hotel before I found out I was pregnant. It was a 'mistake' but it was a good mistake and, in any case, being pregnant at 19 wasn't young for where I grew up. I was very pleased because my dad had shared with me how it was his dream to stay alive for his grandchildren. It made me happy knowing I was doing something for him. When my mum and dad lost my wee brother, I felt they were always missing that baby and I wanted to give them a grandchild. I thought it would make them feel complete.

Both Mum and Dad were over the moon with the news. Michael's parents were a bit displeased – or maybe 'disappointed' is a better word – because they were Catholics. Having sex before marriage wasn't the right way to do things. We didn't tell the bishop I was pregnant because I was in the process of converting to Catholicism. Instead, we brought the wedding forward six months so I wouldn't be showing!

Both sets of parents put in what they could for the wedding although mine didn't have much. I bought a white dress in the sale – it was really quite boring looking, but as I turned over the fabric in my hands, an idea popped into my head. I'd recently watched a film called *My Stepmother is an Alien* and I loved the backless wedding dress which had a big heart cut out in the back. So I turned to the woman in the shop. 'The dress is a bit ugly, but it's all I can have money-wise. This is what we are going to do,' I said confidently. I knew exactly what I wanted. 'Who's your seamstress? I need a meeting with her.' The woman disappeared into the back of the shop to get her colleague. Meanwhile, I got my sketchbook out, and I started drawing what I wanted. My fingers came alive as I drew the dress I'd seen in the film. I wanted diamante stones around the heart. I stood back and admired what I had done. I had created something beautiful and it felt amazing.

'I can't do that,' the seamstress said, shaking her head. 'How's the dress going to hold up?'

'Of course you can do it,' I insisted. My can-do attitude took hold. 'Just put a clip here at the top and a clip here at the bottom and put that inside my dress to help support my boobs,' I said as I drew pads and an underwire. I built a bra into my wedding dress. It was the first time I'd designed a bra. The seamstress thought I was nuts. But it worked. The outfit started out as the most ugly and plain dress you can imagine and I transformed it.

I was proud of my creation and couldn't wait to show my mum. I was heading to the dress fitting when I got the horrible news – my mum had gone into hospital. She'd slipped a disc in her back and could barely walk. She was going to be okay but I was so upset that she wouldn't see my dress. She was my mum, I wanted to share those moments with her. The day before my wedding my mum was still at the Royal hospital and it looked like she wouldn't be able to see me walk down the aisle. I was getting upset and anxious because I needed her there. Obviously, I was more emotional than normal because I was five months pregnant and my hormones were going crazy.

On the night before my wedding I was crying in my room. My mum was still in hospital and I didn't know what was happening. I was young and I felt scared. Suddenly I heard the front door open and then my mum's voice. I ran out to see her hobbling into the lounge. 'I wasn't going to miss your wedding, was I?' my mum said, carefully lowering herself onto a chair. I burst into tears. My mum and dad meant the world to me.

'I'm pregnant, I'm scared, I don't know what's going to happen,' I cried.

'Try not to upset yourself,' my dad reassured me. My dad was always upbeat no matter what pain he was suffering himself. The truth was, I was afraid to leave my parents' side. I'd stayed every night with my mum and dad since I was young. I hadn't even spent the night at a friend's house. I was thinking, Who is going to look after my mum and dad? What happens if my dad gets sick again?

'This is not going to be my room any more.' I sniffed, as my mum tucked me into bed.

'It will always be your room,' she comforted me. I tried to get to sleep but my brain was going at a hundred miles an hour. I was finally about to leave the East End but I felt like I was abandoning my mum and dad. I heard them go to bed and then I sneaked back to their bedroom.

'Can I sleep here tonight?' I asked sheepishly. I wanted to be a kid again.

'Aye, come on then,' Dad laughed. So I jumped in the bed.

'Right, go in the middle.' My mum nudged me.

I rolled between my mum and dad and I fell asleep feeling safe and loved.

4

IF YOU PUT IN MORE, YOU GET TEN TIMES BACK

*To be successful, the first thing to do
is fall in love with your work.*

'I want to go home,' I sobbed.

'You can't go home because you're married now,' Michael reminded me.

The poor guy – I spent our wedding night crying that I didn't want to be married. We went away to a hotel on a golf course in Turnberry for our second night and I was crying the whole time there. We went to Florida for our honeymoon and I was crying the whole time there too. Michael was very sweet and just tried to reassure me that it was all going to be okay but I was pregnant, emotional and scared about our new life together.

One thing I was happy about was that I wouldn't be going back to the East End. We had bought a tiny flat in Shawlands for £38,000 just before we'd got married. There was only one bedroom, a tiny lounge and a kitchen but what mattered most was that it was in an upmarket part of Glasgow. The houses were old and grand, just like the area in which Michael grew up. There was a beautiful park nearby where you could walk without worrying about being mugged.

We had no money whatsoever, so while we were on our honeymoon in Florida Dad put a roller on a stick, and painted all the walls and the high ceilings from his wheelchair. He never let his disability get the better of him. My mum had made all the curtains and stitched together all the bedding. It was an incredible surprise when we walked through the door.

We had only just settled in and then Rebecca was born on 8 August 1992. She weighed 8 lbs 3 oz. She was so chubby and had jet-black hair. Today she looks like my double but back then she didn't look anything like me. People used to joke she had been muddled up at the hospital. She was the best baby ever, so easy, but I was very young at 20; I just didn't know what to do. I didn't feel an instant connection. Of course I loved her but I felt helpless to know how to cope. My world had changed. Michael went to work at his pensions company and I was left alone with this baby, thinking, Is this going to be my life? I can't do this.

I became quite low. I would stare at her pram and think what am I going to do with her? Other days I would cry constantly, and spend hours on the phone to my mum. It was the first time I turned to food as comfort. Rebecca was asleep one day and I thought, What shall I do? I know, I might as well go and eat. So I ordered the biggest pizza you could imagine from the Italian up the road, Di Maggio's. It was a vicious circle: the more I ate, the bigger I got and the more down I felt. All my friends were going to Ibiza and I was pushing a pram up the street to go to Di Maggio's. I had the baby blues. It's a normal, natural thing to have but at the time I didn't know what was wrong with me and how to deal with it. Eventually, Michael told me I needed to see the doctor. I didn't tell my mum and dad I was going. I felt ashamed to admit I needed help. I remember sitting in the doctor's surgery with Rebecca and feeling so alone.

'I don't know what's wrong with me. I can't stop crying,' I confessed to the doctor. 'I don't know what to do with her.' I could feel the tears building. 'I don't feel I'm a good mum. I don't know how to be a mum.' I broke down.

The doctor told me I had postnatal depression and prescribed Prozac. I didn't instantly feel better but the depression lifted after five or six months. I stopped the medication, I lost a couple of stone in weight and I started to enjoy being a mum.

I think the moment I first felt that bond with Rebecca was when she fell ill with an infection. She had a raging temperature and I had to rush her up to Yorkhill children's hospital. My heart was in my mouth; I was so worried about her. The thought that I might lose Rebecca made me realise how much I loved her. It was the moment when I felt the connection. I grew up a bit after that. These were happy times with Michael, who was a great dad to Rebecca, and I think he felt good being the breadwinner – he was the boss of the family.

As I started to feel better in myself, I remembered why I had moved out of the East End – why we were struggling with money just so we could live in a nice part of town. I couldn't afford to be a stay-at-home mum, but I didn't want to be either. It was my goal to have a job and have a salary. 'You know you don't need to work,' Michael tried reassuring me.

'I am desperate to get a job, I am desperate to learn business and I am desperate to work for a big organisation,' I told him. I'd pulled myself out of a dark place, and I now wanted to shine.

Just after my 21st birthday I saw a job at Labatt Brewery advertised in *The Grocer*. It said I had to have a minimum of three O-levels to be an admin girl to support the sales team. So I lied. I didn't have the qualifications but I knew I was bloody good at selling. I thought, If I can just start at the bottom and show these people, I'll be very successful.

I managed to get an interview. I remember feeling so determined when I turned up that day. I knew what I wanted. I pleaded to the guy interviewing me: 'I really, really want this job. I'll work my ass off, please just give me a chance.' I spoke from the heart. If you speak from the heart and you mean it, you will win people over.

I remember a letter arriving on my doorstep a few days later. I screamed so loudly, the neighbours probably thought, What the hell is going on? I picked up the phone and called Michael. 'I've got the job!' I shrieked. I was going to earn £12k.

'Well done,' he congratulated.

'I'm getting a company car too,' I went on. I was getting all these perks that I'd only ever dreamed of. 'Oh, my god, now I've got a salary we can move house. We can move out of this tiny flat. Let's talk to the bank.'

'Hang on, let's just...' Michael started.

'Michael, can you talk to the bank now and see how much we can get?' I pushed. Once I got on that ladder, once I'd got a taste of it, there was nothing stopping me. I was so ambitious with Michael, it was scary: 'No... we need to move here... No, we need to stretch... We have to, we have to work harder...' That's all I ever did with him – stretch, stretch, stretch.

We moved to another posh area called Mansfield before I'd even got my first pay cheque. We were moving up in the world – we had gone from a flat to almost-a-house. It was a conversion and we had the basement and the ground floor.

When I started supporting the sales force at Labatt I quickly made a name for myself for working above and beyond the hours asked of me. The job was 9 am to 5.30 pm but I spent many nights driving up and down to Aberdeen for promotions. I always believe if you put in more, you get ten times back. I was soon exhausted but I was driven by success – I wanted to get to the top. I kept a book in my bag that I filled with notes of what I wanted to achieve within business and my personal life. *I want a better car… I want a bigger house… I want to take my mum and dad away on holiday.* My thoughts would come to me all the time from first thing in the morning to the nights when I couldn't sleep.

Back then, material things turned me on. I thought that buying a bigger house and having a nice car were the key to happiness – because I'd never had those things. I'd seen Mum and Dad struggle and I thought they would have been happier if they'd had all those things that I was aiming to buy, all those things I was filling my book with. I thought you could fix problems by becoming rich.

We couldn't afford to pay for a nursery so Rebecca was dropped off at my mum and dad's every day. I'd still make time for her when I could. I'd feed her breakfast and do her bath when I got home. I probably didn't have the balance right but I was working hard for her as well. I was doing it to get us a nicer house and I really wanted to give Rebecca the best education. I wanted her to go to private school just like Michael had done.

I wanted Rebecca to have all the things I didn't have growing up. Having Rebecca made me more ambitious. I wouldn't have been so driven if I hadn't grown up in the East End and I wouldn't have been so driven if I hadn't had Rebecca so young. No question.

Within four months I was promoted to a sales role and I kept working my way up. I got a reputation for being able to sell beer that was running out of date. I would do my hair and make-up, visit all the pubs and do deals with the guys. They now say to me, 'Michelle, we didn't need your beer, but you were so nice and we wanted to help you.'

I made sales grow by a factor of four. I was turning Rolling Rock and Labatt Ice Beer into something phenomenal in Scotland. I told my boss I was going to take on Budweiser – and I absolutely kicked their asses.

I think my secret was that I was being very creative, thinking outside the box. I'd organise party nights, I'd come up with deals. We had a budget for entertaining and I came up with the idea of using it to buy fridges. I paid a visit to Sir Willie Haughey, one of the big Scottish entrepreneurs, who is now Lord Haughey.

'You're the fridge guy?' I said. 'Do a deal with me on your fridges and I'll buy a load from you.' I wasn't afraid to approach anyone. Everyone in the company was whispering, 'She's buying fridges – what's she doing that for? She should be using that money to take these pub owners out to the football. She should be wining and dining them.' But I thought, No, everyone else is doing that. So I did deals with the pub owners using the fridges to barter. A fridge was a lot of money for a pub owner so I'd turn up and give them the chat. Just as I'd done when I was an Avon rep.

'Look, your fridge is knackered. You need a fridge for your business, it's a major tool. If you buy a hundred cases of my beer, I'll give you a free fridge.' I did more and more deals. The fridge guy, Lord Haughey, liked me because I was buying all his fridges and he would invite me to the football and said I could bring guests. So I was actually doing a double whammy of selling and entertaining for the same cost.

Did I work my looks to make more sales? Absolutely. I lost even more of my baby weight and I felt great. I was right on my game. I would wear a tight dress with my hair and make-up all done. I would step out of the house in the morning looking immaculate. 'All right guys, how are you doing?' I greeted them with a smile. They wanted to spend time with me because people want to look at and do business with someone who is well presented. They don't want to look at someone whose hair needs washing and whose fat is splodging out the side of their dress. A huge smile gets you a long way. If you smile, someone will smile back at you. If you're miserable, then someone will be miserable back. It's just simple, common sense.

I'm not sure what Michael thought of my tight dresses; he didn't really mention it. Saying that, he probably knew I would give him a mouthful. I remember we were going in to see the bank and he tried to stop me. 'You can't dress like that, you are showing too much cleavage,' he said.

'I'll dress how I want,' I snapped. Just because I was going to the bank I didn't see why I had to dress down. I've always liked to look glamorous, ever since my mum used to dress me up for my elocution lessons. I've always believed that women should use their femininity. All these debates about 'Should we dress up for meetings?' Absolutely – guys do it, so what's wrong with a woman doing it? You should always make an effort because it shows you'll make an effort in your work as well.

I was promoted again and again. I worked my way up through so many positions. I was head of sales for Scotland by the time I was 23. My salary had jumped from £12k to £40k, which was a hell of a lot in 1995.

As soon as I was earning decent money I did whatever I could to help my parents out. I bought them extravagant gifts like a state-of-the-art TV. I took them to Majorca, hired a disabled apartment and I paid for all the meals. It filled my heart with joy to see my dad enjoying the sunshine.

I was slowly ticking off my goals. But as soon as one goal was ticked, another ten would appear in my notebook. I worked so hard, night and day. At the weekends I wasn't supposed to work, but I would still work.

Labatt was where I first discovered the 'zone'. It's a term I came up with to describe my new mindset. The zone is where you are at your most powerful because your brain is switched on so you are achieving so much more. It's also a very calm place – you know what you are doing and when you have to do it by. Staying in the zone is hard. It takes determination and courage. It's almost like what boxers do; they go into the zone to win. Training your mind is vital for success because once you get your mind sorted out you can do almost anything you want to do. You've got to spend time training. Tell your mind, 'No, don't give up. We are going to do this and it's going to be hard but if we make it, the results and the rewards will be incredible.'

The more successful I became at Labatt, the more arguments we had at home. Things started to go a bit pear-shaped in my marriage around that time. It was nothing serious, just that

Here I am posing for a few early photographs with a cheeky grin!

I was born in the Gallowgate area of Glasgow. It was quite a poor area of the city but I have some great memories of growing up there.

[© Urbanglasgow.co.uk]

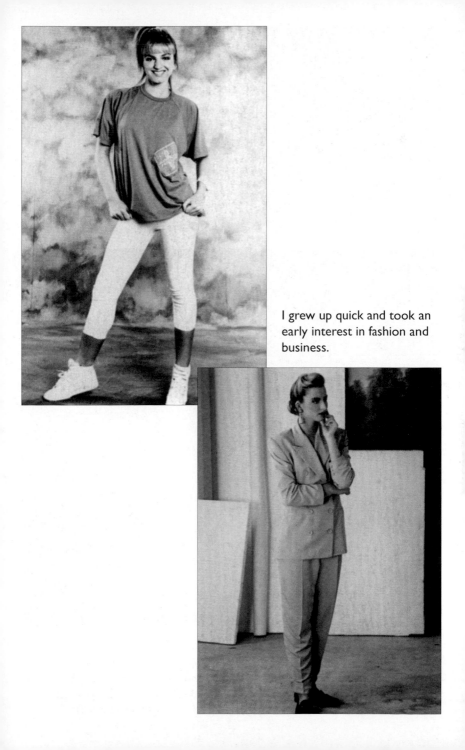

I grew up quick and took an early interest in fashion and business.

Family is the most important thing in life. My parents were so supportive when I was growing up and trying to set up my career. I'm hoping to be just as supportive to my own family. Here are a few photos of my mum and dad sitting alongside my son Declan (*top left*), my mum and I sitting with my daughter Bethany (*top right*) and my mum and I having dinner together (*bottom*).

My weight was always an issue, particularly during the years when I was married. I was very camera shy in the early years of my career (*left*) and it was an amazing feeling to become the face of my own business years later (*below*). [© Sven Arnstein]

[© Stephen Hughes]

I had a poster of Richard Branson above my bed when I was a wee girl. I always knew that one day I'd get to meet him (*top*). I've had the opportunity to meet a few other amazing people during my career, including Boris Becker (*middle, first from left*) and Eva Longoria (*middle, fourth from left*), and my fellow entrepreneur Peter Jones (*bottom*).

I received an Honorary Doctor of Arts from the University of Hertfordshire in 2010. It was a very proud moment for me and my family.

I unleashed the so-called 'bra wars' back in 2004 when I employed Rod
Stewart's ex-wife Rachel Hunter as the new 'face' of Ultimo (*top*). Rachel
replaced Rod Stewart's current wife Penny Lancaster (*bottom, second from left*),
pictured here with her husband Rod (*first from left*), Michael Mone (*third from
left*) and me at the Ultimo lingerie fashion show in 2003. *[© Press Association]*

sometimes Michael would make some cutting remarks – silly things that brought me down.

Of course it hurt, but I drew on the strengths I'd learnt growing up and tried to shrug it off. Instead, while Rebecca was asleep I'd put my energy into my paperwork. To be fair to Michael, he probably couldn't get close to me when I was in the zone. I'd become a workaholic; I had to do as much as I could in waking hours. I suppose it must have hurt Michael that I didn't need him as much financially or emotionally. I'm not telling you I'm an angel, because I'm not. But it was a bit chicken-and-egg – if Michael said nasty things about my background then I wasn't going to show him love and attention. If I didn't show him love, he wanted to be nasty to me.

It was just difficult being a young mum, a wife, and having a career.

5

BECAUSE YOU LOVED ME

When you're happy you enjoy the music;
when you're sad you understand the lyrics.

Michael and I aren't getting on very well, I thought, so maybe another baby will solve our problems? I came off the pill and within hardly any time I was pregnant. I don't think I'm alone in having wondered, *Maybe it will bring us together?* A lot of people believe that having a kid will fix things. But more often than not it's like sticking a bandage over a major wound – the wound will reappear if not treated properly.

I carried on working hard. I didn't for one second think that having a baby would jeopardise my job at Labatt, mainly because I knew that I would never ever let a baby be a handicap. A baby isn't an illness – having a baby is like taking a holiday, just a longer holiday. I appreciate that some women can't leave their kids and want to be with them but I knew I could have both.

Of course, it wasn't long before the cracks in my marriage

started to show again. I was having a really bad pregnancy and I didn't feel Michael was there for me. I was in and out of hospital with problems. I had unexplained bleeding and at one point I was scared I was going to lose the baby. I put on a brave face at work but behind closed doors I was crying all the time. All I wanted was for Michael to comfort me, to tell me he loved me, to hug me, but he wouldn't. Or maybe he couldn't. He pulled further away. I would sometimes lie in bed wishing Michael would put his arm around me, pull me close and tell me it was going to be okay. I'd quietly cry myself to sleep just like I did when I was a child, when I was terrified I was going to lose my dad.

I went along to one of his office dos to find the women were flirting with Michael and he was flirting with them. I ignored it but inside I felt awful. They were thin and beautiful and now I was fat and ugly carrying this big baby bulge.

'Why is he being so nasty to me? Why isn't he being caring when I'm pregnant? Why do my friends' husbands treat them well when they are pregnant and Michael treats me like a piece of shit?' I cried to my mum.

My mum told me she thought Michael had two sides to him. 'He's got his good points but he's quite controlling. I don't think he realises how controlling he can be,' she said.

God knows how I managed to carry on working so hard or how I continued putting on a smile with my clients when both my body and my heart were in so much pain. I was always good at putting on a good show though. It was my mum who eventually warned me to stop doing it to myself. I'd had another fight with Michael and I needed her help. 'You need to come over,' I cried down the phone to her.

It was the middle of the day and my mum was helping me out with beer promotions. She had been going around the pubs that morning. 'I'll be right there,' she said. She could hear the distress in my voice. Mum found me on my knees by the radiator in our spare room. I was sobbing uncontrollably and she couldn't get a word of sense out of me.

'I've just had a terrible fight with Michael,' I eventually spluttered.

My mum came down hard on me. 'You need to remember your baby, Michelle. That baby is going to get stressed out with the way you are right now. You need to calm down.'

Things did calm down until four weeks before I was due to give birth – when I got terrible pains down below. I doubled up and fell to my knees.

'Michael!' I screamed. Luckily, Michael was in the house and came running to my side. 'I think I'm going into labour.' I panicked. Michael carried me to the car and rushed me to the hospital.

'It's too early, it's too early,' I was crying the whole way there.

Declan was born a month premature on 30 April 1996, weighing a tiny 4 lbs 2 oz. He lay beside me and I screamed that there was something wrong with him. 'Help, help!' I cried. His heart was pounding through his chest. His wee tummy was swollen.

'He's fine,' the nurse tried to reassure me.

'No, he's not fine, there is something wrong with him, please get the doctor,' I insisted. The doctor came to look at Declan and his face dropped. The next thing I know they were rushing my baby away. 'What's happening? What's happening?' I cried. Declan was put into intensive care in an incubator to help him breathe.

It was just awful when my mum and dad arrived because

it brought back all the pain they suffered losing my brother. Seeing them cry made me even more upset. Michael tried to put on a brave face. We got constant updates from the doctor but he wasn't giving us any hope. The doctor told me he wasn't sure if Declan would live.

'It's touch and go at the moment,' he said as I watched over Declan's incubator. I couldn't take my eyes away from the baby. A few more hours passed before the doctor delivered the news I'd been dreading. 'I don't think he will make it through the night,' he said tentatively. His words were like a javelin through my heart.

'Oh, god, no.' My mum clasped her hand over her mouth.

I was in so much shock I could barely speak.

We decided it was time to get the bishop who married us, Michael's uncle, to come down to the hospital. We had to prepare Declan's wee soul. I can't tell you how awful it was having us all crowded around Declan's incubator, praying, as bishop Mone gave my baby his last rites. He looked so helpless with all these tubes and wires coming out of him. I didn't leave his side all night. I kept playing Celine Dion's 'Because You Loved Me' to him, over and over. I chose that song because I'd heard it so much on the radio while I was pregnant. It was Declan's song.

'Please fight. Come on, Declan, stay with us,' I whispered in his little ear. He miraculously made it through the night. I never left his side, I kept praying for him.

After a week, I wanted a hug from Michael. I needed that contact. Declan's condition was stable so I jumped in a taxi and went home. I turned up unannounced.

'Hi! Surprise!' I said to Michael with my arms open. I was so happy to see him. But he went nuts.

'What are you doing out of hospital?' he yelled.

'What?' I was confused. 'Please, Michael.' I reached out to him.

'Get back there now,' he said. He was just going mental, absolutely mental.

I burst into tears. I was already feeling so weak. 'Why are you doing this to me? I've just had a baby,' I cried.

'It's not all about you. Get back,' he ordered.

I wasn't trying to be selfish. I just wanted to feel human again and have a bit of normality. Maybe it was his way of dealing with the stress and heartache but it was so hurtful. Again, I was reaching out and he wasn't there to grab me.

'I'm taking you back right now,' he insisted, leading me back to the car. He dropped me at the hospital. 'Get out, stay there, and I'll speak to you later,' he said before speeding off.

I couldn't believe it. I was so upset and I felt so alone. I dried my tears and went back to Declan's side. I clasped my hands together and made a little prayer. *Okay, I've got my mum and dad, I've got Rebecca but I want my husband back. I can't cope with the arguments any more. Please look after me and I'll look after you.*

I didn't sleep much. I stayed by Declan's side the whole time. And then it was like the cloud lifted and Declan pulled through a week later. I took him home and for a while things were calm. I was constantly checking up on Declan though. His crib was beside my bed and I would get up throughout the night to see if he was still breathing. My anxiety levels were probably sky-high, although I didn't realise it at the time. Then, as if I hadn't been through enough suffering, I got the news that I'd been made redundant. Labatt had sold out to Whitbread.

I was devastated. I couldn't believe I'd lost my job. The job I'd fought so hard to get. What were we going to do for money? How were we going to survive? We now had two kids and a mortgage to pay with just Michael's salary.

God, are you trying to test me?

Not long after, I got a letter from Whitbread offering me a job with a better car and a better salary. It's funny how what life throws at you sometimes make you realise what's important. I now had a choice: I could keep climbing the career ladder or take the redundancy money – something like £20,000. That was a lot of money back then.

Almost losing Declan had made me anxious about leaving his side. I didn't want to be on the road until late at night any more. I wanted to find a job where I could spend more time with my family. Maybe it was time to start up my own business. Michael agreed I should take the money to enjoy doing things as a family for a while.

Six weeks later I went to a dinner-dance with Michael. It was just a rugby dinner-dance. I was sitting at a table with all of our friends and I had a long black dress on. Underneath I was wearing a cleavage-enhancing bra. It was bloody uncomfortable. The wires were digging into my chest. I couldn't concentrate on what I was saying to people so I excused myself and went to the toilet. It was while I was taking off the bra in the cubicle, that I had a 'Eureka!' moment. I knew what I was going to spend my redundancy money on.

I've found that over and over again in my life I've had to sink to rock bottom before I can reach the top. But every time I come back I reach even higher. I bounce back bigger than I've ever been. When I push that button, *whoosh*, it's turbo-mode.

I returned to the table with a big smile on my face. I turned to everyone and announced, 'I'm going to design a bra.'

They all looked at me like I was nuts. I remember Michael saying that I couldn't even sew a button on a shirt. 'What do you know about bras?' he laughed.

'I've got a pair of tits – I'll figure it out.'

6

ALWAYS DO THE THINGS YOU ARE PASSIONATE ABOUT

*Choose a job you love and you will
never have to work a day in your life.*

'Oh, my god, I need to find these implants!' I shrieked.

'Michelle, we're on holiday,' Michael said.

'I know but I have to contact this company,' I said, shoving the magazine under his nose.

We had used a bit of my redundancy money to go on a family holiday to Florida four months after Declan was born. We were staying in a villa with friends Nigel and Andrea and they had brought their baby boy along as well. I was supposed to be recharging my batteries after all the upset with Declan but I couldn't. I was lost in my thoughts all the time we were there. My idea to design a bra was rushing around in the back of my head. I picked up a magazine I'd seen lying around on a coffee table in the villa and spotted an advert for breast enhancers – or 'chicken fillets', if you like – you know, the squidgy implants you stuff inside your bra to make your boobs look bigger.

The idea was now in my head and I couldn't let it go. I needed to find out who manufactured these enhancers because I knew they were what I was going to invest my time and my money into. These enhancers would be amazing to put inside the bra I wanted to invent. 'I need to find these chicken fillets!' I said to Michael.

I made Michael go to the mall with me. The poor guy, I dragged him into shop after shop, asking people, 'Do you know where you can get these?' pointing to the magazine. I eventually found a store that stocked the enhancers, but they couldn't tell me who manufactured them. I bought them anyway. They were great; they felt like real breast tissue. The drawback was that they were expensive, costing £150.

I spent the whole two weeks driving and phoning around stores, trying to track down the manufacturer. I was like a dog with a bone. Honestly, I think I drove my friends mad. But I was hit with a wall of silence. No one would tell me. Which wasn't surprising, really, as the details of a supplier are the unique selling point. Guarding them is the way stores make their margins. I came home empty-handed but of course that didn't stop me. I was determined. I spent another two months trying to track the fillets down. I kept phoning stores back in the USA, sometimes the same stores twice. I made up a story to get some answers.

'I'm setting up a shop in the UK and I really want to buy from the supplier. Please can you help me?' I pleaded. It was this wee lassie, over the phone in one of these shops in Florida, that finally told me.

'Yeah, sure, here you are,' she said and she gave me the name. *Yes. Finally.*

I tracked down the guy. He was called Jack Lewis and was based in Miami. It was a family business and they were Jewish. I told him my background with Labatt and how I really wanted to be his distributor in the UK and Europe. 'Can I come over and see you?' I pushed.

Jack was laid-back and he just said to me, 'Yeah sure, why not? When do you want to come?' *Whoosh*, that rocket inside me took off again.

'In a couple of days,' I told him.

'This is mental,' Michael said, as I was booking the flights for the both of us.

'No, it's not, it's going to be huge,' I said with conviction.

'We are going to have to pay for the distributorship. They won't just give it to us,' he said.

I turned to Michael and said, 'Yes, they will. I'll get them to give it to us.'

We left the kids with my parents and we flew back to Florida the next day. I went into the meeting and we chatted for hours. Jack was maybe about ten years older than Michael and we all got on really well. We became close – Michael and I went out for dinners with Jack and his wife, Val. Jack told me he couldn't give me the exclusive rights to his breast enhancers for the European market.

'You'll need to pay for that,' Jack explained. I needed to haggle. And it came naturally.

'Look, I don't have the money but I'm telling you I will sell these like nothing else,' I blagged.

'I can't, Michelle,' he said.

A few days later, I was about to go to the airport for my return flight and I decided to try one last time. I wasn't taking 'No' for an answer. 'Please, Jack, don't make this a wasted trip. All I can say is that I promise you that this will be the best thing that's ever happened. I will turn this business into something huge in the UK and Europe.' And then I came down hard. 'But I'm not doing it unless you give me the distributorship. I'm not wasting my time. I will get them into all the papers and magazines and then people will buy from you as well, so what's the point in me doing the hard work for you to see the rewards? And I tell you what, I'm going to do them anyway. I'll just find another manufacturer.'

Jack went very quiet but I could tell I was winning him over. Michael was staring at me like he wasn't sure if I was his wife. He'd not seen this side to me before. 'Look, what have you got to lose?' I smiled. 'You're not selling it in Europe at the moment anyway.' Jack looked me in the eyes. I knew I had him. 'So give me it and I'll make it worth your while.'

Michael was staring at me, Jack was staring at me and then Jack drew in a deep breath. 'Okay, deal,' he said.

We left for Glasgow with the distributorship and we hadn't paid a penny for it. The agreement was we would buy them at a certain price with my redundancy money and sell them at a certain price. So Jack would make his margin, I'd make my margin and the stores would make their margin.

I came home feeling incredible. But as with all my victories I didn't just sit back and enjoy it. For me, it was like, what next? What can we do now? I'm always driving forward. So I hit the ground running. The first thing I did was register my company. Michael suggested it was named after him, his initials – MJM International – in 1996. I then hit the phone.

It was my aim to stock these enhancers in every store. My

sales pitch was that I had these revolutionary silicone gel pads that would enhance your boobs by two cup-sizes. I got appointments everywhere – thinking back, I don't know how I managed to get all those meetings. I came to London with a case containing samples from Jack. The gel pads were very expensive at £150 retail and that meant I had to target high-end lingerie boutiques like Rigby & Peller. I sold the pads everywhere and then I started the PR. I wrote my own press release, sent it to all the newspapers and the publicity just kept coming and coming.

The enhancers were called Monique but they were soon nicknamed 'chicken fillets'. The local papers wanted to interview me. Who is this woman who has launched these 'chicken fillets'? And then the Scottish national, the *Daily Record*, wanted to interview me. Seeing my name in the paper I'd read since I was a kid was a really big deal. They now call me the 'bra tycoon' but back then I was a 'businesswoman'. My mum and dad would ring me up and tell me how their neighbours were talking about me, how Gran had read about my success in her tea leaves. Dad said his friends down the pub had read about how I'd started up my own business. Sadly, I also heard a rumour that people were saying, 'It won't last', but I shrugged it off.

I worked from a desk in my bedroom with Declan's cot by my side. Michael was still in pensions but he would do the books and the legal stuff for me at the weekends and in the evenings. He wasn't that interested in the creative side of things but he liked the trips. By then I was earning 'okay' money, more than at Labatt, but nothing to set the world on fire. I was always thinking, What's next?

Keep going. Must keep going.

I thought back to my 'Eureka!' moment in the toilets at that rugby dinner and dance. My dream from day one had been not just to sell a Monique-style enhancer but to invent a bra with a Monique built into it. The problem with the current product was that they were solid silicone. I'd been wearing them myself to promote the brand and they were weighing me down. I wanted to design a liquid silicone version that I would incorporate into a bra.

I convinced Jack to give me the contact details of the chemist who had designed the Moniques. I was straight-talking – I told Jack that I'd still buy his breast enhancers but that I needed to earn more money, that I needed more products and I had this idea for a new bra. We had become really good friends and I'd earned Jack a lot of money in the space of a year so he was happy to help me out.

I'd gone from finding the store that had sold them to finding the guy that distributed them to finding the guy who had invented them – in a laboratory in Germany. I was now about to find out what it was like to design my own bra.

By now I'd also gone from the desk in my bedroom to my very first office, thanks to a grant I'd won from the Prince's Trust. I was back in a rough area of Glasgow – Hollybrook Place, near Govanhill – but it was a start, and it was a five-minute drive from our house. The grant of £5,000 got me my first computer and some furniture for the office, a mezzanine over two floors. There were desks at the top and I stored all the boxes at the bottom. It was like a mini-warehouse down there.

After I spoke to the German scientist over the phone, he sent me sacks of silicone liquid gel to look at and over time refined the composition to my specifications. It took about a year to get the gel right and then I had to design the gel into the bra. I cut up old bras and sewed the gel sacks into the fabric but it wasn't giving me much of a polished look. So what did I do? I applied for the job as the distributor for Elle Lingerie & Nightwear for the UK.

'You're nuts, you're mad,' Michael said. I guess he was enjoying the calm after the storm in our relationship and didn't want us to do anything that might rock the boat. But I had to rock it if I wanted to take things to another level. I knew that I needed to find out more about manufacturing to make my invention a success. A job at Elle would open doors because getting distribution rights would mean I could get to know the manufacturers personally. And besides, I needed a job like this to fund my project.

'No, I'm not mad. We need more turnover, we need to investigate more options,' I reasoned.

Tons of people went for the Elle job but, bloody hell, I got it. I couldn't believe it. I didn't mess around. I was quick to ask the bosses if I could visit the factories that were making their underwear. I explained my interest as 'research'. The bosses said, 'Okay, you can go and visit them.'

You beauty, I thought. I was in. I was going to find out exactly who was right to make my bra. Michael came along – he liked the trips! We flew out to Portugal and met up with factory owners. I kept asking, asking and asking, because if you don't ask, you don't get. I was constantly building relationships. I was networking like hell – networking at events staged for women in business. And all the while I was making incredible business for Elle. I was selling their bras and nightwear everywhere. I got them the best sales they had ever recorded in the UK. Again, I did above and beyond my job description – my role was just to sell rather than do their marketing or their PR but I helped with the photo shoots and the brochures.

I became really friendly with the owners of one particular factory in the north of Portugal. It wasn't one of the largest factories, but it was big enough with lots of sewing machines and cutting rooms and all the rest of it. I turned up with my silicone gels and showed them what I wanted. My fingers came alive as I sketched the bra. It was the same magical feeling I'd had when I'd designed my wedding dress nearly five years earlier. I told them the shape I wanted. I picked out the microfibre fabric I wanted. It was good having Michael with me because I didn't understand the money side of things and that was where he came in.

I was working all the hours God sent, but I was still taking Declan with me into the office. Mum would sometimes take him away for a few hours to give me a bit of respite. I'd then pick Rebecca up from nursery. I was basically multi-tasking to get whatever I needed done so I could also be a good mum and wife. It was really difficult but what kept me going were my dreams. I believed if you think big, then big things will happen. I kept dreaming about being the most successful businesswoman in the country. I kept dreaming about having a multi-million -pound company. I kept dreaming and dreaming. Every night, I would lie awake, notepad beside the bed. I'd wake up and make more notes.

'Go to sleep,' Michael would say. But I couldn't, my mind was buzzing.

I wouldn't have achieved any of the work if it wasn't for my mum and dad. They looked after the kids all the time. They did everything. My dad packed the chicken fillets from his wheelchair, working really hard. He came in every single day. I'll never forget when we got our first fax machine. Dad was staring at it like it was from outer space.

'Dad, that's a fax that's coming in,' I explained.

He looked gobsmacked. 'Where's the hole in the wall?' he asked.

I burst out laughing. 'What are you talking about, Dad?'

'How's someone sent that fax through? Where's the hole for it to come through?' He thought someone had delivered it through the brickwork like a letter through a letterbox. I tried to explain, but he shook his head in disbelief. 'I don't get it, I don't get any of this,' he said, throwing his hands in the air. I couldn't stop laughing.

It was a really happy time having my family all together, all around me. And I think Dad was happy because he was working again. Dad was popping pills every day to keep him alive but he never let the strain show. I was making money from Elle, I was making money from the chicken fillets and what did I do?

'Michael, we need to buy this house,' I pushed. I'd spotted a beautiful, five-bedroom house with a mock castle parapet in an even posher area than the one in which we lived – Newton Mearns. It would be our first stand-alone house. It would be our castle!

'We are not doing it, no way,' said Michael.

I stood with my hands on my hips. I wasn't budging. 'No, we have to do it. We will stretch and we will manage. Let's just do it.' I guess a lot of people would have been terrified to make that move when they were unsure of what the future had in store, but I've always been a massive risk-taker, I've got balls of steel. Michael is a very safe person. He's clever with numbers in an analytical kind of way. I'm the creative one – the entrepreneur. But Michael didn't come up with the idea of chicken fillets and he didn't wander around the stores trying to find breast enhancers. There would have been something wrong with him if he'd come up with that idea! He didn't design a bra or work with Elle Lingerie, but he was highly intelligent: he understood the legal stuff, the accounts – all the areas I wasn't good at or interested in.

I not only pushed for the house but I also bought a brand new Audi that I leased through the business. I also hired a nanny to help take the pressure off my mum and dad. Then I stood back for a moment and thought, Wow, Jesus… We are living in this beautiful house, I've got my own office, I've got a new car, I've got two wonderful kids, things are good with Michael… I'm on my way to the top.

I was close to getting my final prototype back from the factory in Portugal when I found out I was pregnant again, in December 1998. It wasn't planned, but it was a nice accident, shall we say. Because I was an only child I've always wanted a big family. I'd grown up watching my friends muck about with their brothers and sisters and I wanted what they had. Some people like being on their own and they love 'me' time but I hate my own company. Michael was happy with the news because he was very much a family guy.

I'd barely had time to celebrate when another box of samples arrived from Portugal. I remember it being a horribly cold January day. I whacked up the heating in my house and tried the bra on. 'Bloody hell! This is incredible,' I squealed.

The bra was plain white and quite ugly compared to what

we design now, but I thought it was the best thing since sliced bread. It was so comfortable. It gave a natural cleavage rather than looking like you'd just stuffed your bra with toilet paper. It was so smooth, so natural. When you bounced up and down, it bounced with you. It looked like real breast tissue. I knew this was it. I jumped up and down and phoned everyone to come around and try it.

'I've only just gone and done it!' I said to my mum. I was over the moon. I had different sizes in the box and I gathered all my family and friends into my bedroom to get stuck in. I remember my aunty trying it on and my mum trying it on. My best friend Ilene gave it a go. They all said, 'Wow'. Good thing Michael was at work as our house was full of semi-naked women jumping up and down!

I watched the smiles on their faces and I broke down in tears. I had put three years of hard work into making this day happen. Michael had been telling me to get on with my sales career but I knew that it would be worth it in the end. The breast enhancers hadn't been mine. Elle Lingerie hadn't been mine. In order for me to break through and make a big name for myself, I had to invent something of my own.

7

THE BIGGEST BRA LAUNCH IN HISTORY

If you really want something, work really hard,
take advantage of opportunities, have a can-do attitude
and never give up – you will find a way.

I was panicking.

We were £480,000 in debt. Our house was acting as security to the bank. I'd given up my distributorship at Elle so I could focus on my dream. Everything was riding on this bra I had invented being a success. I needed to place an order or we were going to be homeless. The question was this: should I take the prototypes around all the independent boutiques? Throughout my life I've always looked at the bigger picture. So I thought big. What's the most famous department store in London? Which is both prestigious and trendy? Where would be the best place in the UK to launch my bra?

Selfridges.

I'll never forget that day I turned up at the buying office just off Oxford Street in London. I was pregnant with Bethany and

I begged to see the lingerie buyer. I told the receptionist I had the best bra ever. She said, 'Do you have an appointment?'

'Er, no,' I said, confused. I was used to the beer industry where you just turned up to somebody's pub, they greeted you with a smile and would ask if you want a whiskey at lunchtime. From beers to bras – I thought you could do the same thing.

'No, you have to have an appointment,' she said in this very posh voice. 'What's this about?

'My name is Michelle Mone. I'm from Glasgow. I'm pregnant with my third baby. I'm £480,000 in debt. It's taken three years of my life to invent this bra. It's the best cleavage bra in the world and Selfridges need to stock it,' I blurted.

'I'm sorry. It doesn't work that way. You have to send in your prototype and we will get back to you if we like it,' she cut me dead.

I didn't have time to wait. 'Please, I can't go home, I need to sell this bra,' I begged.

She eventually took pity on me and phoned the buyer. The buyer came out. I remember her name to this day – Virginia – and she was Canadian. 'I've heard you don't have an appointment. Can I help you?'

I told her the same story, with even more urgency. 'Please, try it on. What size are you? I've got all the sizes here,' I said, holding out my carrier bag.

'Well… I'm a 34B.' She was taken aback.

'Great, please try this on,' I thrust her the prototype.

She obviously felt sorry for me but she had rules to follow. 'I'm sorry, it doesn't work like that. You have to send in your prototype. We have a selection meeting and we will call you if we are interested.'

I started to cry. 'Please, I can't go home,' I sobbed. Tears were dripping down my face. I was crying through fear of being in so much debt and from exhaustion.

She panicked. 'Do you want a seat? Do you want a coffee?'

'Uh-huh,' I sniffed.

'Okay, just be careful about the baby.' She got me a coffee and then I tried one last time. Virginia caved in. 'Okay, I'll try it,' she said. She came out five minutes later with a massive smile on her face. 'Oh, my god, this bra is incredible! I'm buying it. How much stock can I buy? What's the minimum order?'

She asked for six months' worth of stock. I couldn't believe it. The problem was, we had run out of money. How were we going to place orders with the Portuguese factories in time for a summer launch? We had a listing in the best department store but we didn't have the stock to give them to sell. Can you imagine?

Throughout my life I've always got to *there* and thought the job is done, but it's not. Then I have to get to *there* and then when I get to *there* I have to get *over there*. That's the whole story of business. Don't think just because you've got an order, that's it. That's only the beginning.

'The banks won't give us any more money. We can't remortgage our house again,' I cried to Michael. I felt the weight of the world on my shoulders. But instead of the pressure crushing me, it made me want to fight harder. I hadn't gone all this way and put everything in jeopardy to give up now. I needed to think outside the box. 'I've got it,' I suddenly screeched. Michael looked nervous. 'Oh, my god, I've got it! I know where we are going to get our money from.'

I remembered reading in the papers about a Scottish entrepreneur who had just sold Sports Division business for

£300 million. He had grown up in Dundonald, Ayrshire – a rough area like mine. This guy had started off selling trainers from his van. 'It's just like my story!' I said. 'He's going to see himself in me, and give us the money.'

I remembered chatting to the guy in the unit next to my office, George, and finding out he was doing some artwork for Sports Division. I charged on around there. 'George, this is really important,' I said. He looked up from behind his desk. 'You are doing work for Sports Division, aren't you?'

'Yeah, we did a point of sale for them,' he said, confused about where this was going.

'Right, okay, do you know Tom Hunter?' I said.

'Yeah, well, I don't really know him, but everyone wants to know him,' he rattled.

I steamrolled in. 'How can I get to him?'

'Oh, I think that will be quite difficult.'

'No, I need to get to him.'

So he gave me the details for Tom Hunter's friend, Ian Grabiner, who now runs Arcadia Group, the high street retailing giant taken over by Sir Philip Green. I practically sprinted back to my office and picked up the phone. I managed to get through to Ian and I gave him the chat. 'Ian, I've got this incredible idea for a business and I've got this order from Selfridges,' I sang down the phone. I was unstoppable. 'I need to see you. Please, just give me half an hour of your time.'

I had a meeting with Ian and he introduced me to Tom Hunter. Tom, who is now Sir Tom, was exactly like his picture in the paper. He was bald, with a grey goatee beard and looked very dapper in a blazer worn over jeans. He gave off an air of confidence and success. He had such a presence and I was in awe. Michael came with me but he let me speak. He didn't have much choice! I was fighting for my life again. 'We need the money to make the order. We can't deliver to Selfridges in five months,' I explained. 'I swear I will make this brand the biggest brand in the country, I'm going to take on Wonderbra. Just believe in us.'

Michael chipped in too – but we were faced with two extremely clever businessmen, one of whom, Tom, had just sold out for £300 million. It was to be a seriously steep learning curve for both of us. Silence filled the room. I could tell they were chewing the idea over. Tom was the first to speak. 'I want to look in the whites of your eyes,' he said.

To any normal person that would have sounded weird. But it reminded me of the East End. I used to eyeball people to work out what their next move was. It was how you read people. So I looked straight back at him.

'Okay, darling.' He grinned. 'You've got passion. We'll help you out.'

I wanted to scream. Michael's mouth fell to the floor. Tom and Ian were going to invest £200,000. In return, Tom got 20 per cent of the business and Ian got 5 per cent.

I made Tom and Ian a promise there and then. 'I'll never let you down. I will make you money,' I said. We put the order in with the Portuguese and I got cracking on the marketing. I didn't even have a name for my bra yet.

I worked with a marketing agency recommended through the Prince's Trust. I sat for hours with the designer. She came up with loads of names. I came up with loads of names. 'Ultimate' was one, but we couldn't register that because it was an actual word.

'Boost?'

'Nah,' I dismissed it as tacky.

'Ultima?'

'No, I don't like it,' I said.

'Ultimo?' I suggested.

Ultimo! The word just rolled off my tongue. The translation of this Latin term is 'the end'. I interpreted that as the end of looking for bras for my customers – that this is *the* bra. I just thought it sounded very Italian and glamorous.

Then we started to work on the logo. 'I want something curvaceous, that mimics a bust,' I directed. 'You know the Nike swoosh? I want something like that, that people will recognise everywhere.'

She drew a 'U' but it wasn't right. We worked on it for hours until we got it just so. No sooner had I registered it as a brand than I started sending prototypes to film companies, designers, stylists…everyone and anyone who might be able to use it and give us publicity.

We planned the launch at Selfridges for August 1999, well before I was due to give birth. We were going to sell one design in both black and white. We had no pictures, no marketing and I only had £500 left for the launch of the bra. How do you launch a product on the global market when you are competing with the likes of Playtex and Wonderbra? I was still frantically trying to come up with a solution when my waters broke. Can you believe it? Four weeks before the launch in Selfridges and I was going into labour. And what was more, my labour lasted for an agonising 28 hours.

Bethany was born on 1 July 1999. She was tiny, weighing only 5 lbs 4 oz, and she had white blonde hair. She was born on the day Scottish Parliament opened. She had to spend a day in intensive care for observation, but it wasn't anywhere near as serious a situation as it had been with Declan. I went back to work two days later. I had to – my house was up for security to the bank, I had new business partners and I had too much riding on this launch.

I can't describe how I felt as Michael and I packed for the big day. My emotions were a cocktail of nerves, excitement and hormones going crazy from having just given birth. I had my foot on the pedal and nothing could slow me down. We booked ourselves into a Travelodge for the night before the launch, leaving the three kids with my mum and dad.

As we were getting ready to leave for Glasgow airport, I got a call from Tom Hunter. 'There's a jet waiting for you at Prestwick airport.'

'Sorry?' I said.

'Get on my jet,' he said casually.

'Get on your jet? Sorry, what did you say there?' I thought I was hearing things. Okay, so I had gone up in the world – I was now living in a five-bedroom house and driving an Audi, but this was unreal. We headed for Prestwick.

'Oh, my god,' I squealed as we stepped onboard. 'It's just like the films,' I said to Michael. Carpeted floor. Massive leather chairs. There was so much room I didn't know what to do with myself. Shall I sit in this chair or that chair?

'Would you like a glass of champagne, Mrs Mone?' The air hostess carried out a tray with two glasses of bubbly. *Is the Pope a Catholic*? Tom treated me like a princess and it didn't end there. We arrived in London to be picked up by a chauffeur-driven car. *Ring ring*. It was Tom again.

'You know how you booked a Travelodge?' he said.

'Yeah,' I replied, still recovering from my private jet experience.

'The driver is going to drop you off somewhere first. I want you to see something,' he said mysteriously. The driver pulled up outside a hotel opposite Hyde Park.

'This is the famous Dorchester! Oh, my god,' I said, staring up at the grand Mayfair hotel. 'Jesus, this is where they have high tea and everything.'

I was awestruck. This was the pinnacle of everything I had dreamt of. I pulled out my camera, just like any tourist. The driver came up behind us and cleared his throat to get my attention. 'Mr Hunter has booked you in here tonight.'

'Us? You're kidding? No way,' I spluttered.

The manager approached us with a key card. 'Mr Hunter has asked me to show you to your suite,' he said politely.

'Oh Jesus Christ.' I cupped my mouth with my hand.

I'd never seen a room like it in my life. Big lounge. Big dining room. Big four-poster bed. Huge bath. There were flowers, chocolates and champagne. I stared at it all in disbelief. A suite would have cost us £10,000 plus for one night.

Michael was from a different background to me but even he was shocked. I phoned my mum and dad, screaming. 'Mum, you'll never guess what's happened!' I screeched.

'Calm down, calm down.' Mum tried to get some sense out of me.

'I'm in a suite in the Dorchester. I'm taking pictures. I can't believe it.'

Remember I'd just had a baby, but that didn't stop me jumping up and down on the bed like a big kid. 'Calm yourself down, Michelle,' Michael laughed, tugging me back to earth.

That night my thoughts soon turned to the next day's launch. I couldn't sleep a wink. I kept turning over and writing in my notebook. We'd spent our last £500 on hiring 12 actors to dress up as plastic surgeons and picket Selfridges. The message was, 'You don't need a surgeon, this bra is the answer to your dreams.' I kept imagining how it was going to turn out. Was it the best way to spend the money? Too late now. So much was riding on this. There was nothing Michael could say to me to get me to switch off. I was wired. I woke up with butterflies in my stomach. We jumped in a taxi and headed down to Selfridges to meet Tom in time for the launch.

'Oh, my god.' I turned to Michael in disbelief.

The plastic surgeon actors were blocking Oxford Street, waving banners and chanting 'Ban the Ultimo bra, ban the Ultimo bra.' When I say they blocked the road I'm not kidding – one of them even lay down to stop the traffic. The 'surgeons' were carrying kidney bowls as part of their outfits and people threw money, thinking they really had lost their jobs. The story swept across all the news desks within 15 minutes and the next thing I knew, Sky News, BBC and ITN were on the scene. I remember standing outside the department store in my massive maternity gear. I was leaking milk out of my lime-green shirt when the presenter for Sky News came up and asked if she could interview me for the 6 o'clock news.

'You want to ask me questions for the TV?' I stammered, overwhelmed by what was going on. I felt like a fish out of water.

'Yes,' she said, bemused.

'Oh, no, you need to ask my husband.' I backed away. I was camera shy back then!

Michael didn't want to be on TV and told the lady she needed to speak to me. 'She's the one who designed it,' he said proudly.

'What do I do? Where do I look? Is it live?' I spluttered.

'Hang on, I need to find a new shirt,' I panicked, pointing to my milk-drenched top. Selfridges found me something to wear and I did a row of interviews there and then. I was scared at first but after the tenth I started to feel natural in front of the camera.

Meanwhile, Tom Hunter was trying to get my attention. 'Michelle, Selfridges has sold six months' stock in five hours.'

'What?' I yelled across the commotion.

'They've sold out of bras,' he shouted. Selfridges had never seen anything close to it apart from the Furby toy craze at Christmas. Strangers cuddled me in the street, saying, 'You've changed my life, I've got boobs!' It was the biggest ever bra launch in Europe. It cost £500 and I got PR worth £52 million.

I had literally just stepped into my office back in Glasgow when our new employee, Angela, handed me the phone. 'There's an American woman on the line for you.'

'I don't know an American woman,' I sighed. I was completely exhausted.

'It's Barbara Lipton, she's the president of Saks Fifth Avenue, New York.'

'Yeah, right, that will be my friend Ilene winding me up,' I snorted. Ilene and her husband, Bernard, were probably our closest friends. They lived next door to Michael's parents and I'd known them since I first started dating Michael. Ilene was 15 years older than me and had become a sister to me. We'd had a spell of winding each other up because of this radio show that was going on at the time called *The Wind-Ups*. I picked up the phone and said, 'Ilene, what is it?'

'Sorry?'

'Look, stop with your phony American accent,' I went on.

'Do you know that Julia Roberts is wearing your bra in *Erin Brockovich*? The film premiered in Times Square last night,' she went on.

It was too much to take.

'Look, enough! I've been up breast-feeding Bethany all night. I've got cracked nipples, I've got cabbage leaves in my bra, now piss off,' I snapped.

I put down the phone, and then a fax came through with the crest of Saks Fifth Avenue, saying: 'We want to launch Ultimo. I couldn't understand your Scottish accent, can you call me back?'

I was mortified that I'd told her to piss off. Of course I called her back! Barbara told me she wanted to launch my brand in all of her 54 stores. We'd hit the big time. I sat for a moment and reflected. The reason Julia Roberts was wearing my bra was because I had sent prototypes to wardrobe people, stylists and celebrities. I must have sent out 200 bras and Julia Roberts' stylist happened to pick one up. Apparently the stylist had designed a bra for Julia Roberts using parts of Ultimo. So that was a major lesson: never wait for people to come to you; you've got to go out there and get the opportunity yourself.

8

RAGS TO RICHES

Never forget the ones that matter.

'Oh, my god! I've been invited to tea at the Palace with Prince Charles,' I screamed, waving the gold-embossed invitation.

Michael and I had become millionaires overnight. My bras were selling everywhere from Debenhams to John Lewis and we were about to launch in Australia and Canada. Prince Charles invited me to join the Scottish board of the Prince's Trust. Tony Blair nominated me for the World Young Entrepreneur award. I won businesswoman of the year, designer of the year, export brand of the year... you name it, I won it. I was in the *Sunday Times* Rich List as the third richest in the under-30 category in the UK – I was a millionaire by 28! Millionaire, in terms of the company value.

We didn't splash out though – at first. It was amazing that when I put my card in the cash machine it no longer spat it out with a 'F-off'. Yeah, we bought a flash car, a Bentley GT Sport, and I had an extension built onto our house to double its size, but when your business starts flying, you don't get time to stop and party. It wasn't like that. I was run off my feet trying to meet all the demand for Ultimo. I was constantly setting more goals. More targets.

And I was as nervous as hell when I was invited to have tea with Prince Charles. I got that same feeling I had when meeting Michael's parents for the first time – I was out of my comfort zone. I may have moved to a posh part of Glasgow but I was still an East End girl.

'Here are three notepads I want you to get signed for family and friends,' Mum said. She was so excited for me.

'Mum, Prince Charles is not going to sign your books,' I sighed.

'Well, I'm not going to watch your kids on Saturday night, then,' Mum bartered. She crossed her arms in defiance. I took the notepads to keep her happy.

I was very nervous when I arrived at Clarence House, on the Mall, but I composed myself. I was *me;* I wasn't going to be something I'm not. Michael wasn't invited because it was me who originally got the grant from the Prince's Trust. He was now working full-time for Ultimo and looked after the finance, manufacturing and operational side of the business. Michael took on the title of managing director although I think he found it hard to see me take the spotlight.

It was a really intimate gathering; there were only a handful of us there. I remember sipping from a beautiful, posh fine china cup and thinking, My Gran would love this, because she was always into tea and reading leaves. And then this guy came over with a tea strainer. What's that for? I thought. I had no idea at first. I smiled politely as he refilled my cup. I went to the toilet, and it was so posh. Even the toilet paper was different.

I suppose it was a dream come true. I had a flashback to July 1981, to the street party we'd had in the East End when Charles and Diana got married. We'd blocked off Bathgate Street and I'd hung the bunting out of the windows. I was only ten, but I remember bossing everyone around and knocking on doors to see if our neighbours had any tables to spare. We filled the street with long wallpapering trestle tables, covered with red, white and blue crêpe paper. We had a TV in the street – someone's tiny set with the cable running out of the window. We all crowded around as we watched Diana walk down the aisle. What a fairy-tale! And now here I was having high tea in Clarence House next to St James's Palace. I felt like I really clicked with Prince Charles. He was so interested in how I managed to start up Ultimo. He asked me what I did with the grant from the Trust.

'Well, I bought my first computer.' I smiled. It was like talking to a normal person. Prince Charles thanked me for joining the board and he asked what I felt the next generation of entrepreneurs needed. I reflected on my rollercoaster ride over the past three years. I told him that start-up businesses need mentors, someone whose shoulder they could cry on. I guess I felt like I hadn't had a shoulder to cry on when things had become tough. I'd bottled my stress up inside.

My mum and dad had been a massive support, which is why they were the first people I wanted to repay. I've never thought that I work every day for *me*. I've always felt I'm responsible for my mum and my dad and my three children. Mum and Dad had just moved into a bungalow seven minutes down the road. Dad needed a bigger bedroom so he could move around in his wheelchair, so I paid for a massive extension. I bought my mum a car. She was doing the ironing when I turned up at the house. I casually put the keys on the ironing board.

'Mum, there's something outside for you.' I smiled.

'What do you mean, what do you mean?' She started panicking.

'There are the keys.'

'Oh, my god, what have you done?' She ran outside. 'Whose is that?' She pointed to the brand new flash car.

'It's yours, Mum, I bought you it.' She burst into tears. It was very emotional.

After the launch in America, we got another phone call from a woman called Linda Wachner, president of Warnaco, the most powerful lingerie company in the world. Another American wanting to talk to me. Angela passed me the phone.

'Hi, I'm Linda Wachner,' she said.

'Oh, yeah, what can I do for you?' I asked, casually. 'Would you like to buy some Ultimo?'

'No, I want to buy you,' she blasted.

'Sorry?'

'I want to buy your company. I'm coming over to see you tomorrow. Do you have an airport in Glasgow?' she said.

'Yes, we do have an airport. We do have electricity as well,' I joked. I was laughing but she wasn't laughing back. 'I can't do tomorrow, I'm afraid. I'm taking Declan, my wee boy, to the hospital.'

'I need to come tomorrow,' she said.

'Well, I'm sorry I can't see you. I can see you the next day.'

'Okay fine,' she said.

'I'll pick you up from the airport. What flight will you be on?' I said.

'I'll be there at 2 pm and my tail number is...' and she reeled off some digits.

'Tail? I've never heard of that airline,' I said innocently. It was her private jet of course.

I didn't need to pick Linda up as she arrived at my humble offices in a convoy of three chauffeur-driven cars. She stepped out of one of the vehicles with a toy dog under her arm. It was called Ebit. I've since realised that her dog was named after a financial term relating to the way you value your company before interest and tax ('Earnings Before Interest and Tax'). She marched into our office without a 'Hello' or a 'How are you?'

'I want to buy your company,' she announced to Michael and I. She was in her 60s with perfectly coiffed hair and an entourage of guys.

'Well, I'm not for sale,' I said, taking offence at her aggressiveness.

'Now, listen here. People dream about me arriving at their door,' she said.

'Sorry, I don't know who you are.' I crossed my arms.

'We are the biggest lingerie company in the world,' she explained and went on to offer a deal. Linda got all the way up to £19 million in her bid for Ultimo. There was a moment when I thought, Should we just take the money and run? Michael and I looked at each other. It was Michael who finally sent her packing. He was the money guy and he knew Ultimo was worth much more.

'No, we are not interested,' he told her flatly. I felt like our lives had turned into a movie, only I didn't recognise the woman playing me. I suppose I couldn't believe it was real because it was so far from where I started. I couldn't quite believe I deserved it. Some evenings, when Michael was cooking for the family, I would go upstairs and have a moment. I remember sitting on my bed and crying as I hugged my pillow – just like I used to do when I was eight years old, sleeping in my parent's cupboard. I felt alone and lacking in confidence.

I felt guilty for being successful. *I'm not meant to be where I am because I'm supposed to be in the East End, struggling. I was born to struggle*, I sobbed. I woke up every morning with the fear of failure knotted in my stomach. But that's what kept me going.

When it came to the first Christmas after Ultimo launched, I splashed out on Michael and the kids and I had a thought. Christmas should always be a happy time and it was never a happy time for me growing up. We didn't have money for presents and then my dad got sick and we spent the festive period around his hospital bed or across the road in the Chinese. It's a time that should be happy but it's often a worrying time for a lot of people. They don't get to enjoy it because they have to think about money for presents and food.

I got in my car and I drove to the Costco and the Cash and Carry and I filled my boot up with toys and stuff. I then drove to the East End and delivered as much of it as I could. I didn't tell anyone I was coming, not even my family. I knocked on the first door with a bag full of presents. A guy answered. He thought I was doing door-to-door sales at first. 'We don't have money to buy all that,' he said, closing the door on me.

'No, you don't understand, I'm just leaving it with you,' I explained.

'Why?'

'Because I just want to,' I said handing him the bag. I could hear children in the background and it made me smile.

A few people recognised me, some of them were shocked and some people just closed the door in my face. But I came home feeling like I'd made a bit of a difference. Me giving them presents wasn't going to change the world but I believe you should try and do something every day that helps someone out. I don't think successful people should be successful if they don't give back.

When I got home I walked into each of my kids' bedrooms in turn.

'Night, darling,' I said kissing each on the forehead. I would never ever go to bed without kissing my kids goodnight. I'd check all their plugs were off, check the window was securely closed and check whether they were too hot or too cold. I would do that every night because that was what was driving me – my love for my family.

I may have missed out on so many things with my kids because I've been working, but it's because I wanted a life for them that I never had.

9

COMFORT EATING

Keep on fighting.

'What are you doing?' I screamed.

Michael picked up the plate full of spaghetti bolognese and hurled it across the room.

Smash.

There was pasta and sauce dripping down the wall.

'Calm down,' I cried. He stormed out of the room. 'Michael, Michael,' I yelled. I broke down in tears. He'd left me to clean up his mess. Again.

The arguments had become horrendous after Michael joined the business full-time. We were invited to every event and every dinner-dance. I smiled my way down the red carpet but inside I was dying. The problem was supply and demand. Half a year or so after we launched in Selfridges, we started to get major stock problems. Nothing was happening in time. We would get the publicity, sell out, but then we couldn't deliver for months because there wasn't enough stock. The phone rang off the hook – 'Where can I get my size? Why can't I get my size?'

With hindsight, it was obvious that problems were going to arise with the company. Michael had never run a business before; he'd always worked for someone else – in pensions, for example. He'd never had any manufacturing experience, and I was just the creative side of the business. Everything that could go wrong did go wrong. We had fabric issues and cup size issues and there wasn't enough space in the factory machine rooms. Ultimately, the factories weren't being managed properly. Lingerie is one of the most complex manufacturing products. It takes approximately 26 components, of which the fabric is just one, to make one bra. So all 26 components have to come in at the same time to start the production line.

Business is not just about launching a good idea. That's the easy part. The difficult part is keeping up with the demand. Not having enough stock is a problem. Too much stock is also a problem because it ties up money and cash is king. So you have to get a right balance. No one ever gets it right, no one can be Mystic Meg all the time, but we got it so badly wrong. We then got into bed with a production guy who left Elle to become a consultant for us. It didn't work out. There was problem after problem – it felt like two steps forward, a hundred back.

Tom and Ian were left wondering, What the hell is going on?

We were delivering only half of what we should have been. We could have sold ten times more if it wasn't for the problems. We had customers complaining and we were getting negative press. Suppliers warned, 'If this was any other brand you wouldn't still be in our store'. Debenhams said, 'Do you realise, we have never had any other brand let us down like this? Get your act together.'

Stores phoned Tom and it was causing him a lot of grief. Tom and Ian were silent partners at the end of the day but Tom was getting hassle like he'd never had in his life before. It got to the point where Tom and Ian said, 'Enough. Enough of this nonsense. We are now taking control of this.'

Tom and Ian brought in Richard Caring, a multi-millionaire, who had made his money in fashion and retail and would later buy into restaurants and nightclubs. He had factories in the Far East supplying M&S and British Home Stores. They needed his help because Caring was the top expert in manufacturing in the country. It wasn't about money for Tom and Ian because what Ultimo was making was a few Mars Bars' worth as far as they were concerned. It was about respect, because we were embarrassing them.

'I'm sending over my man, tomorrow,' Richard Caring told Tom. They were very close because they had both worked in the same industry – Richard was the best and most successful manufacturing guy in the country.

A guy called Balu, from Hong Kong, arrived the next day. He was Richard's business partner. 'So what the hell is going on here?' said Balu. 'You're manufacturing in Portugal? Are you off your head? No one ever goes to Portugal.' He threw his hands up. Michael and I looked at each other like school kids being told off. 'Let me take it to Hong Kong,' Balu insisted.

Tom proposed a deal with Ian. They would give Balu 15 per cent commission to take on the whole production side of things. Michael wasn't happy being pushed to the side. 'I'm doing this. This is my bag,' he shouted.

'Okay.' Tom tried to calm him down. 'You can still be in charge of manufacturing in Hong Kong.'

Michael was taught a lot by Balu, but it took a while for him to get the hang of things. There is so much to a bra: you come up with an idea, then you make a pattern and then you have to grade all the sizes, it's a massive job. By the time another year went by we still had issues. The brand was getting bigger and bigger as we continued to launch all over the world.

I went into a board meeting with Tom and Ian when Tom turned to Michael and said they felt he shouldn't be doing the job. It was the truth. They had given him a chance to prove himself. The PR, the marketing, the photo shoots, the fashion shows, everything is incredible but the delivery is awful, they explained.

Michael tried to shift the blame. They pulled me aside after the meeting and Tom said the same thing to me. 'Your husband shouldn't be doing this job,' he warned me. 'If you want this business to grow, he's got to leave.'

It was a gun to my head and I had no choice. Deep down I knew he was right, but I had to protect my husband. 'How dare you?' I stuck up for Michael. 'How can you ask my husband to leave? He's my husband.'

'This is business,' Tom retaliated. 'And you are letting so many people down.'

I thought about it for a moment. Michael and I were having lots of fights and I knew Tom and Ian were right, but I came from a place where you live your background. How could I sack my husband? 'I'm not getting rid of him,' I said.

'Well, we don't want to come to your boardroom meetings any more.' Tom drew the line in the sand. We kind of lost them after that. And things turned from bad to worse. I wasn't expecting an actual 'thank you' from Michael for sticking up for him, but I didn't get anything nice in return. Instead, our marriage started to crumble.

I'd tell Michael he had to listen to Tom and Ian: 'You need to get a proper production person in. You have to listen to them,' I stressed.

'No, I know what I'm doing,' he snapped. 'What do they know?'

'Well, actually, they've just sold their business for millions. I think they know quite a lot,' I retaliated.

'They don't know about manufacturing, I know about manufacturing.'

'No, you don't,' I snapped.

'It's my business…' he said.

The whole situation was starting to have a massive emotional effect on me. I felt like I was taking a battering. The arguments became horrendous. That's when he threw the spaghetti across the room.

But at the end of the day you've got to do what the business needs – it's not a charity. If it was me sitting in that boardroom and if I wasn't delivering PR, if I wasn't delivering the designs and if I wasn't delivering everything else needed of me, and Tom and Ian had said I wasn't good enough, I would have left. Michael was too proud.

I didn't know how to fix our marriage so I concentrated on fixing the company. *Planning, planning.* What are we going to do? How are we going to get out of this mess? I didn't have the confidence of Tom and Ian any more. They wanted rid of Michael. It was a Libra thing, you know – the scales. How do I keep everyone happy? It was a question of survival. I wouldn't go to bed until 4.30 am, and then I'd be up again at 7.30 am with the kids. I'd get them ready for school, then head into the office.

I started to binge eat to beat the stress and the exhaustion. I'd drop the kids at school, I'd drive to McDonald's and I'd have a full breakfast. I'd then go into the office. I'd eat five packets of crisps and drink ten cans of Irn-Bru and Coca Cola. I needed the sugar and energy to keep me going. I'd drive out to McDonald's again at lunchtime. 'Big Mac, large fries. Large coke please.' Drive back to the office. Have more crisps, more biscuits and more juice. Drive home at night, go past McDonald's: 'McChicken Nuggets Meal and make that a "large".' I would make the dinner or Michael would have made the dinner. I would then eat my dinner and what the kids had left over.

Because I was staying up late doing emails and planning, I'd have another meal at midnight. I grew bigger and bigger. I ballooned from a size 10 to a size 18. Michael would call me names; he'd wake up beside me in the morning and tell me I scared him.

Sometimes I used to fight back, 'Look in the mirror yourself, you tosser!' But then I'd cry as well when he left the room. I lost all my confidence and I totally went off any sort of affection. Our sex life died. It was only sometimes, when Michael was really in the mood, that we'd do it. I'd lie there, he'd roll on top and then that was it, over.

I would simply feel ugly and want to eat more. It was a vicious circle. I started hiding the food. I'd hide doughnuts under the towels in the linen cupboard because I knew Michael wouldn't look there. I put juice under my bed. I stashed sweets in my wardrobe so I could munch away whilst I was getting ready. I was dying inside. I felt so lonely. I would often go downstairs with my pillow and a quilt and sleep in the TV room.

I made sure the kids weren't affected. They didn't hear most of the arguments. Rebecca had just started school but she went to bed early. She had no idea that mummy was sleeping downstairs on the sofa. Michael would never come and find me.

To be fair, when he married me I was a size 8. I was becoming a different person, so I can understand that he was getting frustrated with me.

Sometimes when we'd fight and I felt exhausted, I'd say, 'I promise to lose weight.'

There was one argument in the office, I'll never forget. I'd just had a McDonald's – my second of the day. I dumped the BBQ sauce in the bin and Michael and I went on to have a massive fight. 'Where's the stock? Why do we have all these complaints about no sizes?' I yelled at him. I was so frustrated that people were still screaming for the product but he wasn't handling the supply. Michael picked up the bin and, in front of Angela, put it over my head. The BBQ sauce dripped down my face. I felt so humiliated.

God, it is horrible just thinking back to it now. I suppose what made it even harder was that I kept all of my hurt locked up. I now had a public reputation. What about my name out there? You know, who was this star in business? I was in fear of the press finding out. I was in fear of my friends finding out. I was in fear of being a failure. And I couldn't have it.

So I kept on fighting.

10

BRINK OF BANKRUPTCY

*The brick walls aren't there to keep us out; the
brick walls are there to give us the chance to
show how badly we want something.*

I had a bad feeling about them.

We were standing outside the W New York, a hotel in the American city. We'd just had a meeting with a Canadian couple who wanted to look after the distribution of Ultimo in America. The Saks department store chain had told us we needed a warehouse in America, we needed people on the ground and we needed a distributor.

This husband and wife team from Quebec, Lydia and Paulo, came highly recommended by the editor of an industry magazine called *Contours*. They were so charming. Very smartly dressed, they knew all the right things to say. But something was burning inside. I was using the intuition I'd developed while growing up in the East End. I'd scanned them and I didn't trust them. The couple wanted us to send them all our stock and they wanted to get paid by Saks and then they would hand our earnings over to us. I wanted it the other way around. Their way was high risk for us. My way was to pay them after they sold the stock.

Now that Tom and Ian had taken a back seat, Michael and I were making all the business decisions, but Michael ignored my reservations. We went back into the hotel and did a deal with the couple. It was decided that we'd send them every item of stock – ten months' worth – and gave them credit as well. Not long after, Tom and Ian started asking questions. 'Has Saks Fifth Avenue paid us yet?' asked Tom.

'No, they haven't,' Michael casually brushed him off.

'Well, you better chase it,' Tom insisted.

Michael wasn't getting any answers though, so I eventually picked up the phone. The line was dead.

Oh, my god.

I tried their mobile. It kept going to voicemail. I tried their house but it went to answer phone. *I knew it, I bloody knew it.* I turned to Michael: 'They've run off with our money and our stock.' I shook my head in disbelief. Taken together with our other stock issues, I knew that this could send us under.

'No, they haven't,' he shouted.

'I'm calling Tom and Ian,' I said, panicking.

A massive fight then broke out between us. There was screaming, shouting and we threw things across the office. It was awful.

I ran to my car and I drove down the motorway, tears streaming down my face. I rang Tom. 'Tom, I need to see you,' I cried. Poor guy, there he was, this multi-millionaire, probably having a relaxing Saturday afternoon with his wife and his kids and he's got this woman screaming down the phone.

'Come now, come to my house, darling,' he said as he calmed

me down. I arrived at his mansion in Troon, a blubbering wreck.

'They've stolen the money and the number's gone dead and they've run off with the stock and I knew it. I told Michael outside the hotel, he's told me I can't do it any more. I need to get a divorce and what's going to happen to the business? I can't fight any more,' I blurted out in one breath.

Tom had a special way of calming a crisis.

'I'll support you, whatever you want to do,' he reassured me. 'You're a very special person and you're talented.'

'I'm scared. I'm scared I'll fail on my own,' I said, wiping my eyes.

'The fight you've got inside you is incredible. Don't be afraid. You're a true entrepreneur,' Tom said comfortingly.

I felt deeply unhappy but my business needed me and my kids needed me – I couldn't get out of it now. So I dried my tears, got in my car and went back home. The couple had run off with £1.3 million and six months' worth of stock. All of it – gone, *poof.* They had done what in business terms is called a 'phoenix'. They had taken all the stock and they had transferred their company name into all of their aunts' and uncles' names. We found out they were serial fraudsters and had done the same to four other companies.

We were thrown out of department stores Saks and Neiman Marcus because we didn't have the stock to supply them. Our lead-time was ten months so we could never replenish the stocks quickly enough. We were haemorrhaging money.

And just as I was recovering from that news, I got the scare of my life. It happened after Michael had gone to the football when I was at home with the kids. Bethany was asleep and

Declan and Rebecca were playing in the kitchen. Suddenly there was blood everywhere – over the floor, over the kitchen units. It was Declan suffering a nosebleed. I rushed to his side. He had been having nosebleeds since he was one year old. He'd had his nose cauterised a number of times in the past five years but I'd never seen anything like this.

'Hang on, baby.' I pulled a big saucepan out of the cupboard and folded him over the pan. I phoned an ambulance and Declan passed out on the kitchen floor. 'Michael, Declan's bleeding, you need to come now,' I screamed down the phone. I cradled Declan in my arms. Blood was pouring everywhere. 'Please, God, let him be okay,' I cried.

We were rushed off to Yorkhill children's hospital and I held his hand the whole way. Michael came charging through the doors not long after. All our fighting and all our problems were forgotten. We had to save our boy. Declan had lost so much blood he needed a transfusion. We signed the papers and they rushed him into the operating room. It brought back all the horror of the days after he was first born. I'll never forget sitting by his hospital bed, playing the Celine Dion song again and again, just as I'd done when he was a baby in intensive care. I was holding his hand when he finally came round. He slowly opened his eyes.

'Mum, where's my monkey?' was the first thing he said. He'd had that monkey toy since he was a baby. I pulled it out of my bag, Declan smiled and I knew he was going to be okay. The doctors couldn't explain the nosebleed but he had to stay in hospital for a week. Obviously, at that point, I didn't give a shit about the business; I just cared about my son. But as soon as I knew my boy was going to be okay, it was back into the fray.

We needed money. The losses had become too great. The Clydesdale Bank called in our overdrafts and gave us two weeks to pay the debt before we were closed down. Our house was up for security again. I had 11 different credit cards in my purse to get credit for the business. I was panicking, *panicking*. I was binge eating like you wouldn't believe. I turned to Tom for help but he refused to put more money into the company. Tom and Ian had had enough.

I had an argument with Tom over the phone. I was feeling desperate. 'You're being mean,' I snapped. 'You can help us out.' I called him names, words I now deeply regret. Tom offered to give me half as long as I could come up with the other half. To be fair, I would have done the same thing if there was someone in the business I didn't believe in, but his offer wasn't enough to save us. We were going under. We had a massive falling-out: it's the only fallout I've had with Tom in 15 years and we are still good friends to this day.

Then it was back to fighting with Michael. It was relentless. One fight was so awful that I took a quilt and a pillow and drove to an Asda car park after the kids were asleep and slept in the back of my BMW X5. I felt so low, so alone and so very scared about our future. My dream was collapsing around me. I rang my mum at 2 am, crying.

'Michelle, you are not sleeping in a car park,' my mum said. She came and rescued me and took me back to their house. I used to stay at their house a lot around that time. I've actually blocked a lot of my memories out because it was so bad, so hurtful. It was just one thing after another. *Bang bang bang.* I coped in the way you would expect a woman who has been working full-time, full throttle, since she was 15 – by working even harder. I didn't stop and I didn't let anything in because I couldn't absorb it. Pain was piled on top of pain until I reached breaking point.

One morning I was so exhausted that I opened up the medicine cabinet in our bathroom and I scooped everything I could find off the shelves. I had all the pills strewn across the floor. I took them out of their foils and built a mountain out of them. I didn't know if they were harmful or not. They were all I could find in the cupboard. A real cocktail. *I'm taking them, I'm taking them.* I didn't want to go on any more. Tears were streaming down my face.

On the surface I was this business star, walking down the red carpet and having high tea with Prince Charles but behind doors it was a horror movie. It was a shambles. A complete shambles. I scooped up a handful of pills and brought the cocktail to my mouth.

11

SAVED BY THE BELL

*Be the master of your fate not the
slave of your problems.*

Suddenly I woke up. I had all the pills in front of me in our bathroom but I thought, I can't do this. I don't know if it was God, because I really do believe in God, but I just snapped out of it. I looked at myself in the mirror. 'You silly bitch,' I shouted at myself. Why are you even thinking this? It wasn't like I had a child who died, as had happened to my mum and dad. It wasn't like I had cancer or was confined to a wheelchair, like my dad – it was just money. There is no way you can give up, I thought.

Your family needs you. Your business needs you. You need to fight your way out of this.

So I decided I was going to fight and find a way. I actually don't know how I'm alive today. I know a lot of people go through a lot of terrible things much worse than what I've suffered, but the situation was severe for me. I'm not exaggerating: it was unbelievable how completely my life had fallen apart. But the thing with me is that when I do bounce back, I bounce higher and even more determined than before. Sometimes you've got to fall before you can fly.

I turned things around in my head because – remember? – if you can control your mind, you can do anything. I thought, I'm lucky that none of this has broken me. It's actually taught me everything I'm going to need for the rest of my life. So I racked my brains for a name I could turn to for help. *Who can I call, who can I call?* I could hear the countdown in my head – a loud ticking of a clock telling me we only had two weeks left before bankruptcy.

Suddenly I remembered a networking lunch I'd been invited to four months ago by one of the most powerful guys in the media – Richard Desmond. He was the owner of *OK* magazine, and the *Express* and the *Daily Star* newspapers. There had been only 12 of us in his boardroom and a butler. I sat next to a guy from HSBC bank. I'd started chatting to him: 'Are you Richard's bank manager?'

'You could say that. I'm Sir Keith Whitson, chairman of HSBC Global.' He held out his hand.

'What, you're the boss for the whole bank?' I choked. At the end of the three-hour lunch he gave me his mobile number. At the time I never thought I'd need it, but now the shit had hit the fan Sir Keith was my only lifeline.

I don't believe in luck, I believe in making the most of the resources you have. You make your own luck in life.

I pulled out Sir Keith's mobile number.

'Do you remember meeting me?' I asked, trying to stay calm.

'Oh, Michelle, how are you?' Sir Keith sounded happy to hear from me.

'I really need your help, please, I need you to re-bank us. I'll never let you down,' I begged. I told him we had two weeks left to pay off our debts. I filled him in on the theft, the stock problems and the nightmare that my life had become. Sir Keith told me to stay calm and sent in his team to look at our books.

It was hopeless though – they needed more time. 'We just can't do it, Michelle,' Sir Keith told me. 'We need six weeks to do the due diligence.'

'But I don't have six weeks,' I panicked. I begged our bank for an extension but they denied us.

I'll never forget the morning of the day they were coming to close us down. Michael was in a room with one of Tom's financial advisors, fighting. 'They *can* give us more money,' he was shouting at Tom. I was pacing the room, trying to come up with a solution. And then Michael suddenly picked up his car keys. 'I'm going out,' he announced.

We all said, 'Where are you going?'

'I'm going to get my car washed.'

And he left to wash his car. I thought, How bizarre. Our life was about to go *pop* and he wanted to wash the car. Maybe that was his way of dealing with it. Who knew? Michael was always trying to show he had more power than Tom and Ian. But Tom and Ian had already made it. I think it went way back to when they asked Michael to leave the business.

Tom's financial advisor also left and I was alone, thinking, Is this really happening? *Keep going, must keep going.* I picked up the phone again and made a last ditch attempt to save us. 'Please, please help us,' I cried down the phone to Sir Keith. I pleaded, I begged. But his hands were tied. He couldn't perform a miracle in minutes. It was 4.45 pm on a Friday afternoon in

2002. We had 15 minutes to come up with the money or we were going under.

Michael was just about to tell the staff to clear their desks. 'It's over. We need to tell the staff.' He threw his hands in the air.

'No, it's not over,' I insisted. Giving up wasn't part of my vocabulary.

Michael shook his head and gathered the staff around.

Ring ring. The office secretary said Sir Keith Whitson was on the phone.

'Hello.' I picked up the reciever, trembling.

'Welcome to HSBC,' he said.

I punched the air with joy. We were back in business. 'I promise you, sir, I'll never ever let you down,' I cried. That bank saved my arse and we've been with HSBC ever since.

I decided to mark the close of that awful chapter by moving office. A bigger team had evolved – we had separate departments for design, technical aspects, marketing and PR, finance, production, warehousing and logistics and I needed somewhere to put them all. I picked an open-plan office in Govan. I wanted it to look and feel like New York because that's where I got a lot of my inspiration from for my designs.

I poured all my creativity into it with the help of an architect called Brian. I said, 'Listen, this is what I want. I want it to be different. I want it to feel cutting edge, but comfortable at the same time.' Brian got me and I got him and it worked out really well. We had big glass bricks on the wall to create that exposed brickwork look. We had real wooden floors mixed with slate. It was out of this world. The office looked like an industrial warehouse from the outside but it was an oasis when you walked through the door. The only downside was being located in a rough area of Glasgow. Occasionally whenever there was a Rangers match, we would get our windows smashed in by drunken supporters marching past.

I'd managed to save the business but I didn't have time to sit back and celebrate. I had to come up with something new – an idea, a PR stunt or an invention that would catapult Ultimo back into the public eye. Ideas come to me all the time. They just hit me – *bang*. I could be getting dressed and then I start thinking, Why the hell is there nothing to solve this problem? But sometimes I have to kickstart my inspiration. I have to go somewhere I can think, somewhere I can breathe. I booked myself into a room on the highest floor I could possibly get at the Four Seasons Hotel when I was back in New York on business.

I played Andrea Bocelli followed by Celine Dion and looked out the window. I knew that I had to keep coming up with inventions for the business to survive. I had to be different to stand out against competitors who had the money that we didn't. 'Why the hell is there nothing to solve this problem?' I said, over and over again, until the answer finally appeared. 'That's it, that's bloody it!' I shouted. I had the first of what would be 15 new inventions.

As soon as I was back in the office I made an announcement. 'We're going to launch a backless body.' I heard a loud groan from the technical staff.

'You can't do it,' one of my designers grumbled.

'Really?' I countered, just like I'd argued over my wedding dress all those years ago. 'Just watch me.' I grabbed a pair of scissors and a piece of fabric. I wasn't a technical person and I didn't go to college but I knew you should never take 'can't' as an answer.

'Put this on,' I said, wrapping the fabric around one of the girls. I cut it down *there*, sewed it *there* and *there*, around *there*, at the top and *there* – *boom*, I had it. Of course, we had yet to perfect the fit, which took the best part of a year, but the concept was there. I was back in the zone. I was filling up my notebook with goals and targets and dreams. I was chasing the money, chasing the lifestyle.

I needed someone to show off the new design. *Bang*. The idea hit me. I needed someone to be the face of Ultimo – I needed a cover girl. I just knew I couldn't afford advertising. I'd done the surgeon stunt outside Selfridges but I couldn't keep doing stunts. So if I get a face then the face will get me the press. I needed someone linked to a celebrity actor or artist. I thought, Well, I've grown up listening to Rod Stewart. His records were playing when I got my dad out of the pub. And Rod had this new girlfriend that everyone wanted to know about. The public was asking, 'Who is she? What does she do?'

I managed to track Rod's manager down in LA and he gave me a contact number for Rod's girlfriend, Penny Lancaster. I spoke to Penny's assistant. 'I really need to meet up with her. Please let me meet Penny,' I pushed.

Penny and Rod were staying at the Dorchester in London and I flew down from Scotland to see them. I thought Rod might buy into my idea because I was also Scottish and Ultimo was obviously a Scottish company. Wow, I thought, meeting a legend like him. Rod was such a cool guy. I gave them both the chat: 'You really need to do this campaign. Okay, my business is only three years old but I'll direct the photo shoot and I'll do it really well. Please be the face of my brand.'

Penny asked for something ridiculous, like a million quid. 'I really don't have that kind of money,' I sighed. I offered her a tenth of that, something like £100,000 for a two-year contract. I remember writing the press release and calling up key editors to tell them what I'd done.

I think everyone now thinks that I was only the wee PR lassie and that Michael ran the whole business on his own. No, it wasn't like that. I did the designs, I did the inventions, I did the shoots, I came up with faces for the brand, I did the selling to the customers and I did the selling out to the stores as well as the PR and marketing. The only hats I didn't wear were finance and production.

Our first photo shoot was in LA in February 2003. We hired a house built by a famous architect in the Hollywood hills. This was a big deal for us because it was so expensive – Penny asked for the top stylist and photographer so the costs mounted up. It was a massive gamble for us, having only just recovered from near bankruptcy. It paid off though, because Penny looked unbelievable when she took off her dressing gown. Her legs went all the way up to under her arms. She was perfect for the brand. She had natural boobs and a fantastic body. She was a stunner, she really was.

Penny modelled pieces from our OMG range – black underwear with diamond Swarovski stone detail. She wore a matching diamond necklace that looked a bit like a dog collar. I'd never directed a shoot before but I got right into it. I'm bad at a lot of things and I've got a lot of weaknesses, like finance, but what I do have is an eye for product, marketing and PR. I discovered

I could also direct. I came up with an idea for the shoot which really did risk Penny's life.

There was a ledge that jutted out from the house and over the cliff. The drop was unbelievable – one false move and you would die. 'Can you imagine standing out there?' I said to Penny, planting a wee seed. 'With your high heels on.'

Penny looked at me, at the drop and then back at me. 'Do you want me to do it?' she said, rising to the challenge.

'It would be an amazing picture, but I'd never risk your life. It's far too dangerous, ' I said.

Penny put her shoes on, the highest stilettos you've ever seen in your life, and she walked out onto the ledge.

'Don't Penny, please don't.' I tried to stop her, but she was determined.

The photographer was shaking. 'I can't do this,' he panicked, adjusting the lens.

Penny balanced on the two-foot-wide ledge that had just enough room for her. You could see the LA skyline behind her. She looked magnificent. 'Okay, hold that pose.' I saw the front page of every newspaper. I worked closely with the photographer, telling him what I wanted. I wanted classy, not slutty. I got such a buzz from creating the perfect picture. That was one of our best shoots Ultimo ever did in LA – it was absolutely incredible. Penny threw herself into it because she wanted to be famous. She knew that shoot would be her launch pad. And so did I and so did Rod.

Michael and I became good friends with Penny and Rod. He invited us to his house in Bel Air after the shoot. It was unbelievable to be sitting in his drawing room, surrounded by all these pictures of Rod with every famous person you can think of. I associated Rod with happy memories of my childhood and the music my mum and dad used to play after winning at the bingo or at the bookies. Michael loved meeting Rod because they were both massive Celtic FC fans. Sitting in Rod's home was like heaven for Michael. Those evenings we spent together were a pocket of happiness in our marriage. Michael was getting attention from Rod, and Penny and I got on really well, and I'd even say we became good friends. It was a nice time because everything was going swimmingly.

Rod took us out to all these fancy restaurants. I'll never forget what happened one night after we'd finished dinner. Penny suggested we go to this place called Hustler. 'Hustler? Why are we going there?' I asked innocently.

'Well, Penny needs to get some toys,' Rod smirked.

'Toys? What do you mean "toys"? Does she need a doll or something?' I was confused. We drove to Hustler, a place that was open late into the night. I'm not kidding, the dildos were so big they nearly brought a tear to my eye. I remember this big black dildo that looked like something you would drill a pavement with. I've never tried anything in my life like this before, I thought.

Rod said I should buy some toys. My cheeks burned red with embarrassment. I wouldn't even know what to do with it. But we all laughed so much in the car about the goodies that had been selected. I looked through everything, reading the instructions on the back of the packets. Michael didn't say a word; we just kept giving each other bashful looks. Our sex life was pretty much non-existent by that point. I had ballooned to a size 22 because I was still binge eating from the stress of nearly going under. Michael didn't want to touch me and I couldn't bear to look at myself in the mirror. I think the only reason I didn't feel self-conscious standing next to Penny was because I was so focused on the shoot and on turning the business around. I returned to Glasgow, buzzing, but scared at the same time.

I had put everything into this photo shoot. I had taken a risk to pay for Penny, taken a risk to go to LA and taken a risk to get the best photographer. The shoot had cost an absolute fortune. But those pictures of Penny on the ledge were gold dust. Those pictures were going to turn Ultimo around.

I was going to show them off at an autumn/winter buyer's convention in Harrogate. I also had the collection samples that we'd spent six months designing. Harrogate was *the* show you had to use to sell your products to the buyers. It's all changed now – in fact, the show doesn't happen any longer – but back then it was a massive deal.

Everyone had left the office for the day. Michael was in Hong Kong dealing with production issues and I packed for Harrogate on my own. I was going to be driving down the next morning. It was a cold and really dark February evening. There were hardly any streetlights outside the office in Govan. My PA and I locked up and I loaded the last box from the collection into the boot of the X5.

'Bye,' I said, waving off my PA. I got into the driver's seat. Suddenly the passenger door opened. A guy with a hoodie was staring at me. 'Oh, hi. Are you looking for directions?' I asked innocently. Stupid me.

Smack.

He punched me in the face. The pain exploded across my cheek. He held onto the handle above the door and used it to swing at me.

Smash. He kicked my ribs.

'Get out of the car, get out,' my PA yelled. My whole body screamed with pain. 'Help! Somebody help us!' she yelled. But no one was around. There were no cars, no one could save me. I knew that if I didn't do anything, this guy was going to kill me. I found my strength. *You bastard.* My future was riding on the contents of the boot of my car. He wasn't taking that away from me. I started kicking him back. Just like when I'd kicked that guy with my roller skates. My nails dug right into his face.

'Get off me,' I screamed.

And then he pulled out a knife. I can remember the blade glistening like something out of a horror film. He held it to my face and I knew he would cut my throat if I didn't give him what he wanted. My PA pulled me out of the car.

The man clambered into the driver's seat and the wheels screeched as he sped off into the night. Smoke was coming off the tyres.

I was in so much pain, but all I could think was, Why did you have to take the car with all the samples that my team had worked on for six months? We've got a show we have to set up for tomorrow and we don't have samples to take orders on. We're not going to get the turnover and, oh, my god, the pictures. The pictures were gone and there was no copy of them. In those days, photos from a shoot were developed onto transparent sheets that could be viewed by holding them up to a light source. Today it's all done digitally but at the time those were all we had – there were no copies.

I fell to the ground, screaming. 'Why? Why is this happening to me?' I sobbed. My PA cuddled me as I cried hysterically on the pavement.

12

WAKE-UP CALL

Look for something positive in each day,
even if some days you have to look a little harder.

'My kids!' I screamed. The police cars had arrived. I was still crying and shaking on the ground. 'He's got the keys to the house. My kids are in the house.' I became hysterical. 'My husband's away on business – it's just the nanny in the house.' I pleaded with them to help. My face was on fire. I had stabbing pains in my ribs.

I can't breathe, I can't breathe.

'Don't worry, Mrs Mone. We are sending a police car to your house right away,' the police officer said, trying to calm me down.

'I need you to take me home,' I ordered.

The police wouldn't let me go home. They sent me straight to hospital in an ambulance. My face had swollen to twice its size. An X-ray showed I had a cracked rib. I didn't care, though. I was fine. I was alive. As soon as I knew my kids were safe, all I could think about was how the carjacking was going to affect the business. I woke up Michael in Hong Kong. He couldn't believe it. But he didn't come home early. He was due in a couple of days and was to join me at the Harrogate show.

The police sent out a helicopter to search for my car. We had an officer guarding our house. It was all over the news. I was in agony, but I still drove down the next day to Harrogate. The show must go on, as they say. We grouped together and I told my staff we would just have to do our best without the actual samples.

I must have looked a right state with a black eye and cuts and bruises. I had scrapes all the way down my face, but I didn't care. I had a job to do. I had to get as many buyers as possible for our autumn/winter collection. I put on a smile. Even when the bank had been about to close us down, I still threw on a smile. But inside all I could think about was those pictures and how they were our advertising for the next six months. We didn't have more money. We weren't insured for them to go missing. Our future had been riding on them.

Ring ring. The caller ID was held. I thought it might be Michael. I answered, hoping he might have got an earlier flight. It was the detective working on the car jacking. 'Mrs Mone, we've found your car,' he announced.

'Oh, my god, you've found it,' I said. I clasped my mouth. My car had a tracker on it but it hadn't been sending a signal the night it was stolen.

'We found it this morning in a garage in Govan,' he went on. It had been hidden, literally around the corner from my office. My bras had been found, scattered all over the neighbouring gardens. I couldn't get them back for the show though because they were evidence.

My heart was racing as I asked him the next question. 'Is there a box in the boot of the car? Oh, God, please tell me there is a thin flat box. It will look like a box for storing paper in,' I went on, rambling.

The detective paused for a moment. It felt like an eternity. My heart was in my mouth. 'Yes, it's in the car,' he said.

I screamed with joy and relief. All the team looked at me like I was nuts. 'Right, the show can now go on,' I said to the team. 'We don't have samples but we do have these incredible pictures of our new cover girl.' I beamed from ear to ear.

On top of that amazing news I could not believe how supportive the buyers were. They had heard about the carjacking – it had been reported everywhere from Sky News to ITN. The national papers reported, 'Michelle Mone, underwear tycoon, was recovering after being battered and robbed in a carjacking ordeal that could adversely affect the future of her business.' Yet the buyers actually placed orders without seeing samples. I'm telling you, there were tears of joy at that show. Michael managed to catch the end of the four-day show and he gave me a big hug when he saw what a state I was in.

My life had changed because of that attack. Even though Michael was back in the house, I still couldn't sleep. I kept waking up in the middle of the night, screaming. I had nightmares about the car jacker holding a knife to my throat. As soon as the police were done taking prints and checking over my car for DNA, I sold it. I couldn't bear to be in it. I got another BMW X5 but I felt unsafe everywhere I went. I became paranoid that someone was going to come at me with a knife. I kept looking over my shoulder.

The police never found the guy, which was surprising

because there was so much DNA to go with – his skin was under my fingernails and he didn't wear gloves, so his prints were all over the steering wheel and inside the car. I couldn't cope with knowing he was out there somewhere with the keys to my house. Of course, I changed the locks but the attack had left some much deeper, invisible scars. I went nuts on the security – I turned my place into Fort Knox. I had locks installed on every single door in the house. Before bed, I'd lock every door, one by one, from the hallway upwards. I had panic buttons put everywhere. I carried spray in my handbag. I got things from the internet I probably shouldn't have got. Honestly, it got to the stage where I had a baseball bat under my bed. I had a knife under my mattress. I had weapons earmarked all over my house. Yeah, it's fair to say I went crazy.

My friends would say, 'Michelle, if someone breaks in and they attack you and you defend yourself, you can be put in jail.'

'I don't care. I'm never going through that again,' I replied. If someone breaks in and they know they shouldn't be there, you should have the right to defend yourself and your kids. I don't think these people who rob you understand the impact they have. It's almost like rape – it stays with you. My PA left not long after the attack. The whole thing really messed her up.

The kids were too young to realise what was going on. Of course, it helped having Michael there – you know, a man in the bed. I don't think he took much notice of the security measures I made. He probably thought, Oh, Jesus, there she goes. Put it this way: he didn't say, 'Put that baseball bat away.' He probably felt a bit safer knowing it was there.

Do you know what hurt me the most though? The rumours that I had staged the whole thing. A journalist told me that people had been saying I had set the robbery up for a PR stunt and asked me if that was true. Can you believe it? Yes, I did put on stunts in the past, like the actors dressed as plastic surgeons, but how could someone in their right mind think I could set up having a guy come and beat me up? The car jacker didn't have gloves on – did they not think I would tell him to wear bloody gloves? It was obviously a junkie, desperate to find what money he could get. It angered me and it still angers me today that someone in the media would suggest that. It really made me think – you fuckers. I started to see the bad side of the press for the first time.

Shortly after the attack and the show I was able to release the pictures of Penny.

The demand for these pictures was already there because the press knew we had signed her but, oh, my god, those shots of Penny on the ledge went everywhere. Suddenly, the press was my best friend. We were in every newspaper and every magazine. The Selfridges stunt had got us noticed but Penny Lancaster took us to another level. Ultimo went *whoosh* – it rocketed. The press went global.

We'd managed to rescue the business and I decided to stage a charity event to say 'thank you' to all those that had helped us. Like I said before, I'm a big believer in working hard, playing hard and giving something back. That was something Tom Hunter always taught me to do. I decided to have the biggest lingerie catwalk show in the UK.

'You have to have it in London,' my team told me.

'Bugger London,' I snorted. 'I'm having it in my home town, I'm having it in Glasgow.'

'You'll never get any stars to come to Glasgow,' they said.

'Just watch me,' I said. I was so determined to make it happen.

I was designing, inventing, selling, marketing and directing photo shoots. I had a team as well, but I was in charge. And then what do I do? I decide to take on a show as well: a fashion show for 2,000 people and a private dinner for 600 afterwards with an auction at the Clyde Auditorium in Glasgow. The date was set for August 2003, less than six months after the carjacking.

This show became a full-time job and, I have to be honest, it almost broke the team, because they were working night and day to make it spectacular. I always say to my team that they should under-promise and over-deliver. If you play it down and produce better results, you'll make people feel that they've got such a good deal that they will pay you ten times more next time.

I ran on nothing but adrenaline. I don't know how I managed to do it. But it was worth it because we raised just under half a million pounds for Breast Cancer, the Prince's Trust, Cash for Kids and Make-A-Wish. It was unbelievable. We had Rod Stewart on the catwalk as well as Penny Lancaster wearing Ultimo. Mark Owen from Take That performed. *Pop Idol* was on TV at the time and some of the finalists sang for us. We had *EastEnders* actors, footballers from Rangers and Manchester United and Celtic boss Martin O'Neill also showed up. Nothing went wrong. But after the show I collapsed.

We'd put Rod and Penny up in One Devonshire Gardens, a stunning boutique hotel. Michael and I had decided to stay with them rather than go home. But I passed out in the car outside. Just collapsed. I was out of it. Michael called a doctor and I was carried to my room.

'You're exhausted,' was the doctor's verdict. I felt sick. It hurt to even breathe. All the stress, all the pressure and all the pain of the past three years had all of a sudden gone *bang*. I felt like I'd been hit by a truck. 'You need to take time out,' he insisted.

Michael was shaking his head. 'Michelle always does this,' he sighed. 'She always pushes herself and I always know what happens afterwards. She comes down to earth with a bang. I could see this coming.'

Michael knew me well. He knew that if I was having a dinner party for friends that I had to make it the best dinner party. If I was cooking on Christmas, it had to be the best Christmas dinner. If I was having a birthday party for the kids, it had to be the best birthday party. If I was doing something for charity, like this show, it had to be the best bloody show. Everything with me had to be the best. I'm all or nothing. I don't say, 'Yeah, I'll do that' and turn up late. I'll put everything into whatever it is I'm doing. I am always pushing for the bigger office or the bigger house.

I've taken so many risks. My mum and dad said to me, 'I don't know how you've managed to sleep at night.' My mum doesn't own a credit card and she's never owned one. At one time I had 11 in my purse, getting credit for this and that aspect of my business. Mum has a wee nest egg put away for a rainy day. She's probably had the same money in her bank for 30 years. Taking risks with money doesn't frighten me at all. Fear for me is getting up in the morning and worrying that I'm going to fail.

The doctor gave me some pills. I went to bed. I didn't even see Rod and Penny off on their jet. I slept through and I woke up – no joke – not the next day, but two days later. It was a warning that I should slow down. I shouldn't have gone back to work so soon after Bethany. My whole career I'd been telling myself 'I can do it' but now I realised my body couldn't do it at all.

13

RACHEL STEALS PENNY'S PANTS

What defines us is how well we rise after falling.

My gran had kept every single newspaper cutting about me. As I came into her flat I saw there were boxes of newspaper clippings everywhere. 'Gran, you don't need to keep all these,' I said looking through the piles.

'Oh, no, I have to keep them because I show the home help people.' The paper almost took over her small flat. 'I always knew you were different. You were always going to be successful,' Gran said, pouring me a cup of tea. 'I remember when you were a wee girl running that paper round. Telling all those boys what to do,' she recalled.

'I think you're right, Gran, second place was never going to be a consideration,' I laughed.

Seeing my gran always pulled me back to earth. I needed some grounding after passing out from exhaustion. Every now and again I felt this overwhelming need to go back to the East

End. Like at Christmas time, when I delivered presents. I needed to reconnect with where I came from, in order to know where I wanted to go. Gran took my hand. 'There you go. That's a wee something for you,' she said, slipping a ten-pound note into my palm. It was ironed and folded neatly into a square.

'Gran, you need to stop giving me this. I actually don't need it. It's fine,' I said.

The business had gone through the roof since Penny became the face of Ultimo and it was around this time that I was first asked to speak at a few charity events. I was shit-scared because I wasn't a speaker. I'd had no media training whatsoever. I remember being about to walk onto the stage at a women's networking event in Glasgow when my stomach turned somersaults. *Oh, my god, I am going to be sick.* I ran to the toilet and threw up my lunch, probably my second McDonald's of the day. I don't know why I was so nervous, but I was.

'Don't be so bloody stupid,' I shouted at myself in the mirror. I wiped my mouth and went out to take the stage. I didn't have any notes, I didn't have any prompts – it just came from the heart. 'Hi, my name is Michelle Mone and I've got a bra business,' I said. I think the audience could tell I was nervous because they started asking me questions.

'Really, a bra business. What kind of bra?' one woman asked.

'Well, I've kind of invented this cleavage-enhancing bra. It's amazing,' I said, as I pulled samples out of a carrier bag. I handed them out for the women to handle and pass around. 'And I've got kids, and I need to get back soon because I'm cooking spaghetti bolognese,' I joked. It broke the ice and everyone burst out laughing. The audience ended up – no lie – laughing and crying and when I finished they gave me a standing ovation.

I had only been on stage for 45 minutes but I walked off feeling shattered. I'd put everything into that speech. I didn't want anyone leaving without saying that I was the best.

I never thought I'd be good at speaking at all but word soon got around the circuit. All the big agents in London and New York signed me up. I'm now the most sought-after women's speaker in the country, I fly all over the world to events. I now get huge money, amounts that I never, ever would have thought I'd command.

There's a general story I stick to when I make an appearance, but every speech is different. And each time, whether I'm to speak to 50 people or 2,000 people, I have to throw up in the toilet first. It's the only thing I'm sick for – public speaking.

Everything was going well by now – except for my work with Penny Lancaster. It was getting more and more difficult to work together. Penny's contract came to an end after two years, but there was no chance of me renewing it. I think people thought we had a falling-out but I just thought, Who can I get next? I'm a businesswoman at the end of the day. I woke up one morning and I thought, Bloody hell, Rod Stewart's ex-wife! Rachel Hunter had been a supermodel since she was a teenager. Ultimo was moving into international markets. It would be a strategic decision to find an internationally recognised new face for the brand.

Bet she wouldn't do it, I thought. Rachel's divorce from Rod hadn't even been finalised yet. *I'm going to ask her anyway, I'm going to track her down.* I remember speaking to Claire Powell, Rachel Hunter's manager. Claire, who also looked after Peter Andre, said, 'Is this a wind-up?'

'No, I promise you it's not a wind-up. Can we meet?' I said.

There was a long pause and then Claire said, 'I'm going to have to call you back to prove you are who you say you are – the *real* Michelle Mone. What's your number?' Claire couldn't believe it was for real. She called me back but still couldn't get her head around what I was proposing. 'Jesus Christ, do you realise what will happen if you replace Rod Stewart's girlfriend with his ex-wife?' she spluttered.

'Er, no, not really.' I shrugged. I actually didn't know. Yeah, of course I saw it as a way of getting publicity for the brand and I knew that in business you have to think outside the box. But I wasn't for one minute using Penny. Penny had been paid for two years' work, and Ultimo had helped her modelling career no end. At the end of the day both sides won. I didn't feel guilty. I never thought for one second it would have the consequences that it did.

We all met up and Rachel was desperate to take on the face of Ultimo because there was a lot of friction going on between Penny and her at the time. The two of them didn't see eye to eye at all. Rachel just said, 'When do you want me?' We signed her at the start of 2004. We kept the whole thing under wraps. We couldn't let the news that I had signed Rachel out of the bag yet.

I was at home, packing for the photo shoot in Miami, when the phone rang. 'Hi, Michelle, it's Richard Desmond.' As in Richard Desmond, owner of the *Daily Express* and *OK* magazine. *How did he get hold of my house number?* 'Michelle, I want you to tell me now...' he said.

'Tell you what, Richard?' I replied nervously.

'Have you signed Rachel Hunter? Is this true?'

Panic. 'No,' I lied. I had no choice, I couldn't let it get out yet. Every powerful person in the media was after this news and it was a mission and a half to keep it quiet. We flew to Miami and we hid from the press as much as we could.

Claire played a big part in the shoot. She took it to another level, bringing on board an incredible photographer called Dan Kennedy who I've worked with ever since. We chose Miami's famous Delano hotel as our backdrop for the spring/summer range. It had a beautiful pool and gardens – everything was modern and white. We hid Rachel under umbrellas so no one would recognise her.

We were standing under the palm trees when Claire came up with this idea to have Rachel model the same backless body that Penny had worn in the Chelsea shoot. 'Both of them in the same outfit for Ultimo. Are you serious?' I said.

Claire gave me a mischievous grin.

'Well, it is one of my new inventions and it has only just been released,' I said.

I had three inventions by this point – the OMG bra, the backless body and the frontless body. I had to keep coming up with new ways of keeping up with my competitors. I thought for a moment. 'Okay, let's do it.'

Those pictures – wow. Rachel, who was 32, had a curvy, sexy figure to die for. Rachel and Penny were both stunning women and they both looked great in the body, but at the end of the day, Rachel was a supermodel. Her calibre and pedigree showed. She was in a different league when it came to working the camera. I was in awe.

'Jesus look how she moves,' I said to Claire, as Rachel struck her poses in the hotel garden. The performance she gave was quite incredible. After we had finished for the day, it was time to celebrate.

'Where are we going tonight?' I asked Rachel. She named a diner in Miami where they only served milkshakes and fries. 'You want milkshakes and fries?' I looked her skinny body up and down.

'Yeah, let's go,' she said, smiling cheekily.

I remember walking in with this supermodel and everyone stared. People kept coming up and asking for her autograph. We sat in a booth with two milkshakes each, fries and a burger. Not exactly what you would expect a model to eat. Of course, I was used to that kind of food. We had such a great time. I suppose the fact that it was a top-secret operation made it even more fun. It was the most I'd laughed in a long while.

I was still excited when it came to writing the press release. Rachel looked incredible and I couldn't wait to show off our new collection. I knew it would make the headlines because she looked amazing and because it was news that Rachel was our cover girl. I released the pictures of Rachel in March 2004.

Boom.

Jesus Christ, to this day I've never seen a launch quite like it.

I had editors telling me they changed their front covers at the last minute to make way for my story. Piers Morgan, who was editing the *Daily Mirror* at the time, rang. 'Am I seeing this? Is this for real?' he gasped. 'I almost fell off my seat!'

I couldn't quite believe it myself. Only two years ago Ultimo had been on the brink of closing down and now we were front-page news all over the world. Some of the papers decided to print a picture of Penny and Rachel, side by side, modelling the backless body. Some of the headlines were quite cutting, like: RACHEL OUTSHINES PENNY AGAIN, said the *Daily Mail*. RACHEL PINCHES PENNY'S PANTS, was another one.

I took a closer look at the picture. 'Fucking hell,' I shrieked. Claire Powell had dealt with the retouching of Rachel's picture and oh, my god, what a blunder she had made. 'Fucking hell, Claire,' I squealed down the phone. She'd photoshopped Rachel's right hand to half the size of what it should be.

'I know, I don't know what happened,' she laughed. It was kind of funny at the time and it detracted from the media circus that was going on. We became really good friends after that.

I didn't get much in the way of a backlash at first. The only thing the papers did make out was that I had sacked Penny. I categorically stated that wasn't true. 'Her contract had come to an end. I did not sack her,' I blasted. In this industry models replace models all the time. It was business. Penny had done a brilliant job of relaunching Ultimo but I was moving my brand onwards and upwards.

14

CHOKING ON MY PROFITS

There is no lift to success,
you need to take the stairs.

The war had begun between Penny and Rachel and I was dragged in. The pair battled it out in the papers – every day Penny would say something and Rachel would respond. I got an absolute battering from the Scottish press because Rod is seen as an icon up there for his love of all things Celtic and of Scotland. I had no clue it would get so big. What started out a publicity stunt quickly turned into a nightmare. I admit, I had made a huge error, one that I would have to live with for the rest of my life.

I need to speak to the press to explain the situation, I thought, panicking.

I decided to do interviews to clear my name. One of the reporters playfully asked me to compare Penny and Rachel to football players and teams. I was still young in business, only

32, and not experienced at that sort of thing. 'Come on, what would you say?' the reporter pushed.

'Well, I don't really know about football,' I said. 'Erm, who's that really famous, really successful star in football? Is it Ronaldo?' I asked innocently.

'Yes,' the reporter smirked.

'Well, Rachel has been a supermodel since she was a teenager so I'd compare her to Ronaldo. Penny was just this wee local model so I'd maybe call her Falkirk Football Club.' I later found out Falkirk played in the Scottish First Division. I had no idea what I had just done until I opened the Scottish *Sunday Mail*. I felt like I'd been punched in the stomach.

'I hope she chokes on her profits,' blasted Rod Stewart. He had given the *Sunday Mail* an exclusive interview and he had given me a beasting. It had been written like I was the most hated woman in Scotland. 'Michelle is a manipulative cow.'

Punch.

'I was told Michelle was a devious, conniving, publicity-seeking son-of-a-bitch. I was told she was a user.'

Punch.

'I don't think Penny has got a single bad bone in her body. But Michelle's entire skeleton reeks of self-interest.'

Punch.

Oh, God, I felt like I was going to be sick. I was, and still am, a big fan of Rod's. I couldn't bear to read his hateful words. I was just trying to make light of the situation. I was just trying to end the war with a bit of humour. I had tried to make everything better but in stupidly shooting my mouth off I had made things so much worse.

Rod went on to say how he still liked Michael; it was just

me he despised. That burned. Michael seemed to love it. He taunted me with it. He might as well have done a victory dance around the kitchen.

I glared at him. You fucker, I thought. I've been the one that put myself through this to save our company and all you're concerned about is Rod Stewart liking you. Okay, maybe Michael was being a bit tongue-in-cheek. But I knew that, deep down, he loved the victory he had over me. All that I wanted Michael to do was to stick up for me, just as I'd stuck up for him when Tom and Ian wanted to get rid of him. I wished I had the same support.

Sales were flying as a consequence of what I'd said but I felt like I had sacrificed my soul for the business to get there. I got such a beating by the Scottish media. I was truly hated for what I'd done. The public in Scotland turned against me. About the only person who liked me as a result of the storm was the chairman of Falkirk football team. He called me to rave, 'This is brilliant! People in America have now heard of us.' He was delighted. At least I had I done one good thing with my comment. 'Do you want to join our board of directors?' he went on.

'No, you're alright,' I said.

I deserved the bad feeling. Rod was quite right to be angry because I had been so stupid. He was right to say he hoped I'd choke on my profits. I do believe you should never regret anything in life because every day is a school day. I didn't make an error hiring Rachel Hunter because Rachel has probably been the best model Ultimo has ever had. Yet I knew I had made an error in saying that stuff about the football teams. I apologised straight away.

I said through the media that I'd made a very stupid mistake comparing Penny to Falkirk. 'I didn't mean to hurt anyone. It was my stupidity. I'm sorry.' No response from Rod. Rod was angry because he trusted me. We'd all had a good time together. I suppose I, in a way, betrayed him. I've since bumped into Penny quite a few times, and it's been friendly, I've said, 'Hello. How are the kids?' We're fine now, but back then, it was war.

My dad took it very badly – he had to watch his daughter be hated in Scotland. 'Just vulgar,' my dad said, shaking his head in disgust at Rod's reaction. Dad had grown up listening to Rod Stewart. It was different for Michael's mum and dad, who never had a record player so they didn't have the same affinity for Rod. But Dad was furious. He destroyed all his Rod Stewart records.

'Dad, what are you doing?' I tried to calm him down.

'That's my daughter he's talking about. I don't want to hear his songs any more,' he said, tossing 'Sailing' into the bin.

I did try and reason with him. 'Dad, this is my fault. This is not Rod's fault. If it was me, I would have defended my boyfriend.'

Dad took a moment. 'It's not the point. He shouldn't be speaking about a lady like that,' he said.

Rod's hateful words had a massive effect on me. I was distraught. I was crying myself to sleep but at the same time kicking myself, thinking I deserved it. Every day I took another battering from the press.

Attack, attack, attack.

I felt very lonely. I needed my husband to comfort me. But Michael was never there. He hadn't been there for me for years, if I was honest with myself. So I turned to food again for comfort. I ate and I cried. I was now putting away four McDonald's a day, 13 bags of crisps and bowls of chips. I was still size 22 and all my trousers had elastic bands. I used to get my PA to hide food for me. I admit I used to get her to cover for me by getting her to lie to Michael.

'How many cans has she had today?' Michael demanded. I'd look at her. Poor thing. She must have felt under the spotlight.

'Only two,' she'd lie.

I sighed with relief. But really the total would have been 15. My sugar intake was obscene. I don't know how I didn't have a heart attack. I was so deeply unhappy but food made me feel good for that tiny moment. I used to get my PA to go to the local Chinese and fetch me a chow mein with chips. I would eat everything on the plate until I felt I was going to burst. I was punishing myself for what I had done, for being unhappy and for being fat.

I looked like a train wreck. My face was so swollen it looked as if someone had pumped me up like a tyre. When I look back at photos of the time I don't even recognise myself. My eyes had sunk into this fat face. My mum and dad were worried about me.

'Michelle, listen to me. You're going to have to get yourself together,' Mum said, sitting me down. 'You're a pretty girl. What are you doing to yourself?'

I burst into tears. I sat on her couch, crying my eyes out. Mum wrapped her arms around me and tried to calm me down, as she had so many times before. She sweetly tried to pick me up by offering me incentives. But I kept the hurt to myself because I didn't want to worry my mum and dad and because my dad was sick. I talked a bit to my friend Ilene, who was still like a sister to me. I didn't reveal much to other friends because someone close to me had been tipping off the media. I was starting to lose touch with knowing who I could and could not trust.

My eating was part of the vicious cycle with Michael. I hated my body to the point that I would never undress in front of him. I would hide behind the wardrobe door as I changed into my big jammies and then get into bed. As you can imagine, our sex life was utter crap. Well, now and again, when he was in the mood, but it was over very quickly. He got his enjoyment. There was nothing about pleasuring me. How could I relax and enjoy having sex when he was making me feel so ugly?

When I stood in front of the bedroom mirror I would hear Michael's words in my head. I hated myself. I don't think anyone had a clue how unhappy I was. I guess the flip side was that the battering I received turned me into the person I am today. Now I don't let anything affect me.

I have developed such a thick skin and I've had to become a completely different person since I started the business. It's sad that business does that to you but it's the truth. Being an entrepreneur is the loneliest job on the planet. Everyone thinks I am tough and powerful but behind closed doors I am actually quite fragile. If a man behaved in the way I did, he'd be hailed a hero. But being a woman means I have to take a lot of shit because women are supposed to be soft and nurturing. These days I think that as long as my friends and my family know who I am, the journalists can say what they like. It's tomorrow's fish and chip paper as far as I'm concerned.

You probably know what I'm about to say – I threw myself into the business to forget what was going on around me. *Fight harder. Must fight harder.* I came up with the idea of creating an affordable bra to sell in a supermarket chain. So we signed a deal with Asda to launch a collection for its George range, called Michelle for George. It went on to become the highest-volume lingerie brand in the country.

It was at that point that Michael insisted we buy Tom and Ian out. Michael had wanted to reclaim our share ever since Tom and Ian said they wanted rid of him. We couldn't afford to do it until now. Tom and Ian were obliging as they'd very much been silent partners since Michael refused to step down. I'm still very close to Tom and I'll be forever indebted to what he and Ian did for Ultimo. It was a risk for them to invest in us and luckily they earned a lot more than the £200,000 they put in at the beginning.

Michael now had full control – and that's when things got really bad.

15

BREAKING POINT

Sometimes you gotta fall before you fly.

Michael and I had been fighting for years. But it came to a head on a flight to Miami in 2005 for our third shoot with Rachel Hunter. It just so happened that my company secretary, David Kaye, was also flying out to see his daughter. He was sitting in front of Michael and me in upper class when a sexy Virgin air hostess came up to us.

'Would you like me to wake you up with a hand massage or a neck massage?' she smiled. She asked Michael first and he started flirting with her. 'I'll wake you up, sir,' she flirted back. I was ginormous at this stage. I felt like I was about to burst. I felt like I was living in a body that wasn't mine and I was so unattractive.

Michael went for a massage that was supposed to last 15 minutes. He disappeared for 45 minutes behind the curtain with her. Nothing happened, obviously, but he shouldn't have been gone for that long. Michael then went to the bar and he talked to the hostess for hours. No exaggeration. Every time I glanced over I felt a knife stab into my stomach. Michael always used to say blondes weren't his type and that he preferred dark-haired girls. The hostess was dark-haired. Michael's comments churned around my head. I hated the air hostess but not as much as I hated myself.

I couldn't take it any more. You fucker, I thought. So I marched up to him. 'That's enough,' I snapped. Michael got the message and came back to his seat. No sooner had he sat down than the hostess appeared again.

'Sir, I've got some extra time, would you like another massage?' she said, smiling sweetly.

'Oh, that would be great,' Michael beamed. I glared at him. What the fuck?

He disappeared again and I couldn't take it. I turned to my company secretary for support. 'This is a joke, David,' I fumed. 'Michael has been at that bar getting absolutely steaming drunk and now he's gone for a second massage.' I fought back the tears.

'Never mind him. He'll fall asleep,' David said, trying to reassure me.

Michael came back to his seat, and I just stared at him.

I had to bite my tongue because our marriage had deteriorated to the point that Michael would blow up every time I said anything to him. It was as if I'd become his worst enemy. So I just looked at him.

He started shouting at me.

I burst out crying and he gagged me with his hand. I swear to god I thought he was suffocating me. *I can't breathe*. I lashed out with my nails to get him off me and he bit my right ear.

I clasped my hand over the ear to stop the pain and when I pulled my hand away I saw it was covered in blood. 'Oh, god, help me,' I cried. David jumped out of his seat and carried me to the toilet. Blood was pouring down my face. I doused the paper towels in water and tried to stop the bleeding. The sink ran red. All of this I did behind a shower of tears.

I eventually left the toilet holding a tissue to my ear. David was waiting for me. He linked his arm with mine and whispered, 'You need to stop screaming. You need to stop now.' I started to sniffle again. 'There will be police at the other end at the airport and you'll both get arrested. Can you imagine the press if that got out? It will destroy your business.'

His words struck fear into my heart. That was the last thing I bloody needed. So I returned to my seat and I did what I did best. I swallowed my pain and just got on with it. But even my skin wasn't thick enough to shrug off what had just happened. I'd never had a physical argument like that with Michael before. I plastered on a smile as we landed in Miami but my hands were shaking. Trembling. I wished I were anywhere but there. 'I want to go back home,' I whimpered to David as we passed through customs.

'You need to put this behind you. We have to do this shoot in two days. You've got so much money at risk. You can't be fighting or you'll put the brand in jeopardy. You have to grit your teeth and bear it,' he advised.

David was right; we were paying tens of thousands of pounds for this shoot with Rachel. I couldn't turn back now, even though I was so unhappy. God, I was so miserable in that marriage.

'As soon as I get home, I'm leaving Michael,' I said.

David sighed deeply. 'Well, if that's how you feel, Michelle. But remember what you've got. You have kids and a business together,' he said.

It was just one of those things. I had to get on with it. At the hotel Michael and I shared a room. There was no escape even though there might as well have been a ten-foot wall between us as we lay in bed together.

Claire Powell and Dan the photographer witnessed a lot of fighting in the van on the way to the shoot. Michael was out of control. He would say I was this and I was that terrible thing. It was so humiliating for him to do that to me in front of everyone. Nobody knew where to look. You could cut the air with a knife. I looked out of the window and imagined I was somewhere far away. The tears burned as I tried to hold them back.

I didn't set out to write a book about Michael and our problems but there is no way I could leave it out. It was absolutely shocking and people around us thought, This is not normal. 'God, that is pure hatred,' several of the team said to me. And it was hatred. I felt like Michael hated me. He absolutely hated me. I supposed it stemmed from when we nearly lost the business. The fighting over money spilled over into our personal lives. The company recovered but our marriage didn't. The only thing I can thank god for is that we shielded our kids from a lot of it.

We arrived on the beach and we started setting up for the spring/summer collection. The first shoot in Miami had been fun. We'd been celebrating and laughing. This set-up couldn't have been more different. I thought Michael was getting quite close – too close – to one of the girls on Claire's team. You know when someone is stepping over the line. Watching them made me feel awful. It was like the plane journey all over again. I couldn't bear it and I had to look away. But I was so lacking in self-confidence that I didn't even say anything. I let him humiliate me. I can't tell you how bad it was. I had to pretend everything was okay but it wasn't – far from it. I knew that I shouldn't be there. I shouldn't have been on the shoot and I shouldn't have been with *him*.

And then Rachel appeared, looking incredible in a lilac lacy bra and G-string. We were both the same age – 33 – but we couldn't have looked more different. I was wearing my elasticated trousers and a massive, floaty shirt, fully buttoned-up so you couldn't see my fat body. I was boiling under the hot Miami sun. Sweat was dripping on my forehead. Rachel, on the other hand, was looking amazing, wearing nothing but Ultimo underwear. I'd never really compared myself to our models before but suddenly I felt so ugly standing beside Rachel.

'Smile,' Dan said as he took a photo of us together. I cringe every time I look at that photo now.

I'd just had Michael fighting with me on the plane and in the van and I had watched him flirting with some girl. I couldn't take any more. I broke down crying. Rachel stopped what she was doing and gave me a hug. 'What's wrong with you?' she asked.

The floodgates opened. 'I'm so miserable,' I sobbed. I couldn't keep up the charade any longer. 'I can't stop eating,' I said. I was finally honest with myself. 'I'm so depressed.' Rachel is such a kind woman. She gave me a gentle squeeze. 'I look at you and you're the same age as me and I'm wearing these big elasticated clothes. I don't know how to get out of this mess. I'm deeply, deeply unhappy and I can't stop eating.' I broke down.

Rachel smiled and told me to stop beating myself up. 'Michelle, look what you have created. Look at the inventions you've come out with. Look at what you've done.' But it fell on deaf ears because I couldn't see my worth. I was blinded. Rachel then turned to me, her tone became serious. 'Why don't you start treating your body like a business?'

Ping.

Business – that was one word I did understand. My eyes opened saucer-wide. It was like one of those cartoons in which a lightbulb goes off above the head. 'Would you ever treat your business like you treat your body?' Rachel asked. This was coming from a supermodel whose business was her body.

'No way,' I said defiantly. 'I'd do anything for my business. I'd die for my business.'

She smiled because she could see I'd got it. 'So why don't you think about *you* for a change?' she suggested.

I nodded my head. 'I'm going to do it. I'm going to lose weight and turn my appearance into part of my brand,' I said.

'That's right,' she smiled 'and when you reach your target, do your own lingerie shoot and show all these women out there what you've done,' she said. 'Promise me you'll do that.'

I shook my head adamantly. 'No way. I could never do that. I'm used to being behind the camera.' And then I laughed for the first time. 'And there's no way I'm ever going to look like you!'

Rachel wasn't taking 'No' for an answer. 'Lose the weight, and do the shoot,' she said.

And that's what I did. I turned my life around.

16

MY 'MONICA' MOMENT

Stop wishing and start doing.

I had a lot of weight to lose but, before I could figure out how to do it, I had a very special event I needed to attend. In 2005 Richard Caring decided to hold a charity masquerade ball in St Petersburg in Russia. Richard was the multi-millionaire businessman once brought in by Tom and Ian to help us and we continued to share an office with him in Hong Kong. By now he was also the owner of exclusive London nightclub Annabel's, and Scott's restaurant in Mayfair.

Private jets ferried a hundred of society's crème de la crème to the ball that was to be held in Catherine Palace. Bill Clinton was also going to be at the ball and he was someone I had always looked up to. He's my idea of a perfect man. I think he's an incredible guy. We landed in the Russian snow on the Friday and were escorted to our rooms. Michael came along too. Things were not as bad as they had been between us on the Miami trip, but there was no love or warmth there. I kept my mouth shut so as not to say something that would trigger an explosion. I guess you could liken it to walking on eggshells – I trod softly.

Knock knock.

I looked at Michael. We hadn't ordered room service. I opened the door to this lady who had a tape measure hanging around her neck and was carrying fabric. 'Hi, I'm your dress maker,' she introduced herself. Oh, my god, we were having our ball outfits especially made up for us. I didn't look at Michael as she took my measurements because I could always read his face like a book. I didn't want to know what he was thinking about my weight.

The following day I remember getting in a lift with other women who were also attending the ball. 'I can't believe the dress she's made me,' one of them whinged. Is she for real? I thought. We were being treated like royalty – a flight on a private plane, caviar and Cristal champagne on tap since we arrived – and these women were moaning.

'It's disgusting,' she went on. *It's a bloody charity event*, I wanted to shout.

This woman was big, like me, so I made her an offer. 'Look, my dress is gorgeous and I really don't mind swapping with you. It's for charity so you can take mine and I'll take yours.' I suggested.

'Where is it?' she demanded. 'I'll come to your room now.'

She just took the dress, she didn't even say 'thank you'. How bloody ungrateful! I didn't say anything though because I've learnt that you have to pick your battles in life.

My new outfit made me look like the maid, but I didn't care as it was all for a good cause. The palace was beautifully done up and the waiters were in Russian costume. The tables and chairs were gold and we drank out of wine goblets. We all got quite drunk while watching Tina Turner and Elton John on stage. Bill Clinton was sitting at the table next to us.

I kept catching myself staring at Bill Clinton. He looked great in a black and gold jacket. I found my courage, thanks to a few glasses of champagne, and approached the former president. He didn't see me coming. 'I've always wanted to say to you that I'm a huge fan,' I gushed. Everyone at his table was staring at me. 'I just… I just… I just… want to be Monica,' I prattled on, saying the name of the intern who had an affair with Clinton in the 1990s. Obviously I meant to say I'd wished I were Bill's wife, Hillary.

Oh, fuck. Did she really say that? Everyone looked at me with disbelief.

Clinton's face just dropped. I'm probably one of the only people to render him speechless. You see; I hardly ever drank alcohol. My weight gain was all down to sugar and grease, not boozing. And it was probably a good thing I didn't when I came out with a faux pas like that! I got dragged off before he could say anything or before I could put my foot in it even further. The experience was highly embarrassing. Luckily, Michael was on another table and didn't hear me shoot my mouth off.

The ball itself was an incredible success – Richard would go on to raise an incredible amount of money, something like £15 million in one weekend for children – what a guy! I remember getting the coach back after the dinner and sitting next to Sting and Sir Cliff Richard when Michael and I started everyone off singing a school-kid chant: 'The back of the bus they cannae sing, they cannae sing…' It's a Scottish thing. I don't think anyone had a clue what I was on about, but they still joined in as we rounded off the night. The ball had shown that there were times when I laughed and had fun. It wasn't all misery but the good times were few and far between.

When I got back to Glasgow it was back to business. I was sitting in a board meeting with the Prince's Trust when all my insecurities returned. I felt like the odd one out – the big, fat, ugly woman in the room. The party was over. I came down to earth with a bang. I could barely hang on until the end of the meeting and then the floodgates opened.

'Michelle, what's wrong?' one of the women asked, concerned.

It wasn't like me at all to behave in this way. I hadn't been brought up to pour my heart out. I'd turned into a bloody weeping willow. 'I want to lose my weight,' I sobbed.

'You need to go and see Jan de Vries,' she said.

'Jan de who?' I asked.

'He's a herbalist, he'll sort you out,' she smiled.

I wasn't going to allow my personal life to spill into my work. It was time to follow up my promise to Rachel Hunter and sort my life out. I went to see Jan in Troon. He was a Dutch guy, really friendly. 'Any time I start a diet, I've finished it by the afternoon because my hunger pangs get too much,' I confided.

Jan listened intently. 'Try these remedies,' Jan said, handing me some bottles.

'Are they all herbal?'

'All herbal,' he reassured me.

Jan handed me four different remedies – I had to put three drops of each in water an hour before eating, three times a day. It wasn't anything like you would get in a diet pill; Jan was using herbs to help suppress my appetite. They were a mixture of all sorts of things including green tea. As soon as I left – literally, while I was in my car driving home – I got into the zone. I was either going to do this well or not bother.

My life changed overnight: four McDonald's a day – stopped. Twelve packets of crisps – stopped. Fifteen cans of Irn Bru – stopped. And I tell you what, I've never had a sip of Irn Bru or Coke since I left Jan's house that day. I remembered what my Gran told me: 'The taste of it will send you back.' Gran wouldn't even touch the trifle at Christmas because she was afraid the small amount of booze in the recipe would turn her into an alcoholic again.

I had an addiction – to junk food – and I knew that if I were to taste it again my life, in terms of my diet, would be over. I swear, as long as I live, I won't drink full-fat Coke or full-fat Irn Bru again. Fizzy drinks ruined my life. Well, I ruined my life, by indulging in food and fizzy drinks and all the rest of it.

I didn't stop eating but I ate less because the remedies stopped me from feeling hungry. Jan's formula rebooted my metabolism and the weight started to come off – 3 lbs every week. I drove down to Troon every week to see him and I let him know how much I was struggling. My body was so used to me feeding it crap that I think it went into shock at first. I was very tired and lethargic for a few weeks until the remedies kicked in and then I started to feel incredible.

I also thought, This is a business opportunity. This is actually making me lose weight. I need to turn this into something. I'd been losing weight for four months when I gave Jan the chat: 'Jan, would you like to go into business with me?'

'Doing what, my darling?' he said.

'Could you put your herbal remedy into a capsule?'

'Yes, of course you can.' He nodded.

I got straight to the point. 'Can we do a business together where it's 50–50?' I thought with my marketing skills, my weight-loss story and Jan's expertise, we could do well together. 'I think there are a lot of people out there who need this remedy. We need to launch this – because it actually works,' I said. I'm always being asked to get involved with businesses and products but I only invest in things I can believe in. I do try everything myself but I usually end up saying, 'No, you're conning people.' I don't mince my words.

'Well, let's give it a go, my darling,' he said.

I drove home and told Michael the good news. 'I'm starting up a business with Jan,' I announced.

'What do you mean you're starting up a business? What are you talking about?' he grumbled. But Michael got involved not long after. He took over the sourcing and the manufacturing side. We eventually launched TrimSecrets in July 2007.

I'd lost almost three stone at this point and Michael had barely said a word about it. I don't think I believed what the scales were telling me. I was so used to seeing a fat me in the reflection that I couldn't see past that image. I remember one typical morning waking up and avoiding looking in the wardrobe mirror as usual. I put on my outfit for the day – a baggy blouse and some loose-fitting black trousers. I met my mum in town and we walked down Buchanan Street in Glasgow where I stopped outside the window of Karen

Millen. I always desperately wanted to go in but they didn't do my size. There was a really nice pair of fitted jeans on display.

'Let's go in and try them,' Mum encouraged.

'I can't, I can't, I can't.' I backed away from the entrance. I had so little self-confidence. 'There is no way I will fit into them,' I said, defeated.

'Let's just have a try,' Mum said. She hooked her arm through mine and led me inside. I felt more nervous going into a high-street clothes shop than standing up in front of thousands of people to do a motivational speech.

I took the jeans into the changing room and my mum came in with me. I couldn't believe I got them on and they fastened too. 'Oh, my god,' I squealed. 'I'm shopping in Karen Millen and I'm wearing a size 16.' I shook my head with disbelief.

'Well done, good for you,' Mum said. She had a tear in her eye. I started crying then too. The shop assistant must have wondered what the hell was going on.

I'll never forget that day because it was the start of my transformation. I developed a style. I stopped shopping in the area for big people in department stores and started shopping in places that suited my own style. I always had a really good eye for design and fabric quality but I'd been too big to do anything about it until now.

I started splashing out on designer clothes. I started to feel good and my confidence grew and grew. Michael noticed the change in me, mainly because I was finally sticking up for myself. When Michael shouted at me in front of the staff, I shouted back. 'Don't speak to me like that,' I told him. I wasn't going to be humiliated any longer.

We were in a room with our board directors and he shouted at me, telling me I didn't know what I was talking about.

Yes I bloody did. 'And you know what you're talking about do you?' I snapped. I used to absolutely hammer him back.

I felt like a new woman by the time I met Bill Clinton again. I suppose I was, in some ways, hoping he might not recognise me after our last run-in! I was invited to speak at a very special event in London alongside some of the world's most influential leaders. There were 2,000 people and it was being shown live on CNN. I was standing backstage, waiting for my turn, when I felt that familiar feeling of nausea. *Oh, my god, oh, my god, it's coming.*

Mikhail Gorbachev was leaving the stage. He was a tiny wee man, I noticed. And I couldn't stop the inevitable. The sick splashed on his shoes. *What are you doing?* The organisers stared at me in disbelief. Gorbachev was horrified. I wanted to die. I had to quickly wipe the saliva and sick off my face because they called my name. *So much for leaving a good impression on another world leader!* But I went on stage and still managed to give the speech of my life.

17

TOO BIG FOR THEIR BOOTS

*People who are meant to be together find their
way back; they may take a few detours
but they're never lost.*

'She's Mariah, you have to wait,' Mariah Carey's manager reasoned. I had been looking for a new cover girl to keep the brand fresh and among the names was the famous singer. Again, I was thinking big and the meeting with Mariah Carey was quite something. It probably will go down as one of my most unusual experiences.

I walked into the Sanderson hotel in London to find they had turned her suite into a swimming pool. What the hell is going on here? I thought. It was a proper swimming pool, a massive blow-up one filled with water. She was making a music video in it.

I arrived there at about 6 pm to talk to her about being the next face of Ultimo. It got to 2 am and she still hadn't seen me. I needed matchsticks to keep my eyes open. I signalled to her manager that I had had more than enough. 'Come on, mate, I can't be waiting here any longer,' I grumbled.

He looked at me like I was speaking a foreign language. 'She's Mariah, you have to wait,' he said. He looked over his shoulder to see what the hold-up was. 'She's having her eyebrows done at the moment. Won't be long,' he explained.

Another hour passed. I've waited for so long now, I thought, I might as well see it through.

'I want a Chinese,' I heard her ask her staff.

'Mariah, everywhere is shut,' explained one of her entourage. They came back with a Chinese within 45 minutes though. God only knows where they got it from.

It was 4 am by the time I eventually got to see her. We were chatting when she suddenly stood up and took her dressing gown off. She was naked except for two butterfly stickers over her nipples. 'What do you think of my body?' She smiled.

God. It's like five in the morning, I can't deal with this. 'Yeah, your body is amazing. I actually need to go home now,' I said. I left pretty sharpish. She was a potential as a face for the brand, but then I thought she was a bit too much.

We did a one-off shoot with supermodel Helena Christensen, but I didn't feel there was quite enough personality there. Blonde models have been much better for sales than dark-haired girls such as her. I'm not sure why that is though.

In November 2006 we signed Girls Aloud singer Sarah Harding. I chose her because I thought she was fun, I thought she was great for the brand and I loved her songs. She was like the black sheep in Girls Aloud and I liked the way she stood out. But when we started working together it quickly became apparent that she was extremely insecure. Probably the most insecure of all the models I've worked with. She didn't have any confidence which is surprising because she looked stunning in her photos. She was in tears before every shoot. 'I don't like my hair that way' or 'I don't like my make-up that way.'

You could tell she was going down a dangerous emotional road. I could spot it a mile away. She was like a rabbit caught in headlights. I felt sorry for her lost wee soul. I comforted her a lot – almost like a sister, I suppose. I even invited her to stay in my house so I could look after her.

I remember telling her off, like a big sister would, on the way to a shoot. We were in upper class to Miami with the hair and make-up team behind in economy. The make-up artist appeared next to us. 'Sarah, can I get you a duvet, darling? Can I get you a pillow?' she said. 'What can I do? Can I tuck you in?' *Am I really hearing this?*

Sarah turned and smiled, 'Yes, could you tuck me in.'

I didn't have time for this. I stood up and told them off. 'What the fuck? I've never heard anything like this in my entire life – you coming here to tuck Sarah in,' I scolded. 'This is lunacy. You,' I said, pointing to Sarah, 'you shouldn't be behaving this way.' I turned to the make-up girl. 'And you… you get back to your seat.' Sarah looked at me like a wee kid. But that was the relationship we had developed. I looked out for her. I was like her sister, her mentor.

It's funny. I think the people around celebrities are to blame for spoiling them when they should be telling them to behave themselves. Apart from a few celebrities, like Rachel Hunter and Michael Bublé's wife, Luisana, most celebs are like kids.

My daughter Rebecca hates the celebrity world. So much so that she didn't care for the idea of Sarah Harding staying in our house.

'Can Sarah have your bedroom?' I asked. Rebecca was 14 at the time and all the wee girls her age were into Girls Aloud. We even had a load of teenagers outside our house screaming when they discovered Sarah was staying with me.

But Rebecca wasn't having any of it. 'No chance,' she said. 'That's my bedroom and she's not staying in it.' And she crossed her arms. She doesn't give a damn about celebrities. I think that's probably because she's seen a lot of drama with the press and me. I ended up putting Sarah in our spare room in the end.

I guess I understood what Sarah Harding was going through because I too suffered from a serious lack of confidence; although that was changing, week-by-week, with every pound I was losing in weight. I was now not just changing my clothes but also my hair and make-up. I was rebranding myself. I was starting to spend money on myself.

I got French manicured acrylic nails. I put on fake tan. I threw all my make-up in the bin and started again. I received some tips from the make-up artists I'd used on my shoots and then I went to House of Fraser in Glasgow and bought bagfuls of new lipsticks, glosses, eye-shadows and mascara. Rachel Hunter even gave me some tips, like how to blend eye-shadow. I had a blow-dry several times a week. The only time I'd had a blow-dry until now was if I was going to a dinner-dance. Now I was getting them done just to go into work and I felt amazing for it. I believed that to be a success, you have to look successful at all times.

I was really changing and Michael hated it. He ripped into me for 'looking fake'.

'You look like Jordan,' he said. 'Fake Jordan.'

'Why am I "fake Jordan", Michael?' I replied, sticking up for myself. 'Your friends' wives have blow-dries like me.'

'No, they don't.' he said. 'They do their own hair.'

'No, they don't,' I said.

I was growing so much in confidence that I decided to appear in the Ultimo brochure alongside Sarah Harding. Under my picture was a message welcoming readers to the Ultimo range. For the first time in years I didn't want to turn away when I looked in the mirror. 'You actually look okay,' I said to myself. I'd always had attention from men before but I used to laugh it off, thinking they must be joking. I never believed they could be chatting me up. Now I believed it because I believed in myself.

I suppose, if I'm honest, I also thought that if I lost the weight Michael would start to be a husband again. But when that didn't happen I filled the void with material things. We were earning lots of money, big money. Ultimo was probably worth multi-millions at this point. I started splashing cash like it was going out of fashion. Jewellery, flash cars, designer shoes and designer dresses. I had a new office built from scratch in East Kilbride. It was massive: the two storeys had glass panels throughout. I designed it in the shape of a breast. I couldn't stop. *What next?* It was always 'What next?'

I designed a house for us – my dream home. I'd grown up watching *Dynasty* and *Dallas*, telling my mum and dad that one day I'd have the mansion with the sweeping staircase. I chose the most expensive postcode in the whole of Scotland

– Thorntonhall, an exclusive village in the countryside of the outskirts of Glasgow. The houses would be worth £80 million if they were in London. It was millionaires' row. Thortonhall was the dream destination for all our friends. I had thought, Give me a few years and we will get there – and we did.

Stretch, stretch, stretch.

It was on my list of things I wanted to achieve and, *tick*, I did it. We'd gone from a two-bedroom flat in Shawlands, to a conversion in Mansfield, a house in Newton Mearns and now this – the ultimate. I designed a grand, sweeping staircase to be made out of walnut wood. The builder had a complete nightmare but I wanted it badly so I pushed and pushed. I also designed a walk-in wardrobe – another item I'd seen on *Dynasty*. All my shoes could be lined up. I wanted lingerie drawers for all my bras and inventions to be neatly displayed in rows just like in a shop.

In total, the house featured six bedrooms, a bar, a TV room, a cinema with reclining leather chairs, a lounge, a dining room and a 30-ft family room. There was even a nightclub out the back. You couldn't have got any bloody bigger. I designed the interior to look like that five-star suite from the Dorchester hotel that Tom Hunter had put us up in on the night before our launch in Selfridges. That night was just magnificent. I really felt that the Dorchester represented a life that I wanted, a life that was amazing, a life that was a fairy-tale. Every piece of furniture was made for the house by Dorchester suppliers at a cost of around £600,000. The master bedroom had a 7-ft bed with a padded headboard, Romano lamps on both side tables and a Sonos sound system.

The house was perfect. I named it Telperion, after a tree

in Tolkien's *Lord of the Rings*. I thought that was my path to happiness – the more things you have, the happier you become.

I couldn't have been more wrong.

18

DIVA BEHAVIOUR

The strongest people are not those who show strength in front of us, but those who win battles we know nothing about.

'Too much salt, start again,' I barked at the caterers. I was hosting a massive party for 200 friends and family in our new house and it had to be perfect. Everything always had to be perfect. *Don't give me all right. I don't do all right. Give me fucking brilliant or don't give me anything.* I wanted people to leave saying the food was incredible and that it was the best party they had ever been to. 'Why has this not been set up yet?' I shouted at the guys putting the marquee together in the garden. I was turning into a real monster – a diva.

It wasn't just the party. Nothing was ever good enough. The hotels I was staying in weren't good enough and the restaurants I was dining in weren't good enough. I once asked to change rooms at the Dorchester because I didn't like the way it was decorated. I found fault in everything. In the same way, I bought more things because I thought they would make me happier. I'd got rid of my addiction to junk food and replaced it with an addiction to buying things – very expensive things.

We had five cars in the driveway at one point, including an Aston Martin DB9 and a chauffeur-driven Bentley Arnage to take me to events. To be fair though, Michael was also very materialistic. He loved the cars – they were like his babies. If I even so much as scratched a wheel he would go ballistic.

Alongside the vehicles I owned 100 pairs of Louboutins and my dresses were £4k a pop. One of the most expensive things I bought was a custom-designed Rolex with diamonds. And even then I found fault – it was a vicious circle – with the watch, 'No, those aren't enough diamonds, send the watch back,' I ordered. I didn't go off the things I bought, I would just think, What's next? The same way I did in business. I thought I had to have all these things to demonstrate my success as a high-profile person. I suppose footballers are the same – they often come from a working class background and suddenly make a huge amount of money.

It first dawned on me that I was turning into an diva one day when my driver took me into town so I could do a bit of shopping. He opened the door for me, and instead of saying thank you, I said: 'You've not parked in those lines straight.' I pointed at the painted parking space. He just looked at me in disbelief. I think he was thinking, You are a witch. I'm surprised he didn't tell me to stick my job up my arse. I stared at him, and he stared at me. Did I just say that? I thought.

Yeah, it's fair to say, I went a bit off the rails in our new house. I used to always dream about having these amazing things, and now I had become like, 'Yeah, so what.' I didn't appreciate what I had and nothing was ever good enough because I was really unhappy. I was in an unhappy relationship and I was buying all these things because I thought it would numb the pain but it didn't.

Material things don't make you happy. A big house and a fleet of cars are not going to change your life. I had a grand house in the most expensive postcode in Scotland but I was at my most unhappy. The fighting with Michael was at its worst. I was covering up the issues because I had kids with Michael and I had a business with him. I was also proud – it would have been embarrassing if it had got out in the press and if my friends knew what was really going on. So I pretended that I had a perfect life instead. I felt so lonely and trapped.

I think my stress and unhappiness also manifested itself in my OCD. I had been obsessive about cleaning since I was a wee girl when I used to tidy up my mum's tiny kitchen. In our previous house, in Newton Mearns, I used to make the nanny follow all of my rituals. Every Friday, she would have to make sure the kids' rooms were spotless. I gave her rules such as ensuring we all had our own ironing baskets. She and the kids all knew that they couldn't put a pine hanger in a walnut wardrobe. But things started to get a bit out of control in our new mansion. I installed four dishwashers because I couldn't bear the sight of dirty plates.

I remember I'd been away for a couple of nights on business and I came home to find the salt grinder had been left out in the kitchen. *Panic.* It made me feel so uncomfortable that I needed to check if anything else was out of place. I opened the cupboards one by one, checking they were tidy and that the labels were facing the correct way. *Relief.* I felt in control again.

I then went from room to room checking that everything

was in order. I had to make sure each pillow was plumped up. I had to check that my wardrobe was organised. I needed to see that all my bras were lined up. Only then would I be able to sleep peacefully. I did it with my kids as well. I'd go into Declan's room and say: 'You do realise the pillow zips are up the wrong way?' And when he was not around, I'd fix it all. Tidying made me feel calm. I couldn't control what was going on around me but I could have control over my wardrobe, and the other small things. I cannot function if I have a messy wardrobe. I often say to people: 'Organise your drawers before you face the world.'

I had lost the plot a bit, but thank god for my mum and dad helping me to spot it. Mum turned up at my house one morning. 'Are you coming in?' I asked, holding the door open for her. My mum peered in and stared down the hallway. Mum and Dad hated coming to my house. My mum is like a white witch. She reads tea leaves, just like my Gran, and she never felt comfortable in my house.

'It's like a show home,' she shivered. The house was perfect. But she was right. Apart from the kids being there, the house was soulless. It wasn't a happy home. I went back to hers, sat down on the couch, and I finally broke down in front of my mum and dad.

'I've got five cars, I've got a massive house. Why am I not happy?' I sobbed.

'Michelle, you are losing sight of who you are. You have always been an exceptionally giving, generous, loving and caring person. What's happened to you?' she asked.

'I don't know,' I sniffed, wiping the tears from my eyes. I felt like a lost little girl.

'Michelle, you've got to remember where you are from, where you were brought up,' Mum went on. 'Only then will you find yourself again.' She was right; I'd lost my identity. 'Your barriers are up, Michelle. You are not letting anyone in.'

I'd toughened up because of all the fighting with Michael. I wouldn't let anyone in. I wouldn't show any emotions. I was in defence mode, constantly. 'All the things you have look like they've come out of a movie. Why are you not happy with it?' Mum asked.

'I'm not happy in my marriage. I don't know what is going wrong. And I don't know how to fix it.' I broke down. Of course, Mum and Dad had known for many many years how bad things were but saying it out loud brought a sense of relief. It broke down a barrier. My nurturing side came out after that. All I cared about was my mum and dad and my kids.

I do believe every day is a school day and, believe it or not, I actually appreciate going through everything I did because I know I'll never do it again. I don't need material things to make me happy. I have also realised my kids don't need the fancy things. They just need my time. Your heart costs nothing. And that's why I thought it was time to write this book – because I've learnt all this.

I started to do a lot more with my kids. I'd cancel going into work if they were ill. I became more relaxed around them – before I was often very tense because I had half my brain worried about business issues. I learnt to leave the company problems at the door.

I decided to confront some underlying issues with Declan – head on. Declan was really struggling at school. He needed help to become more focused on his learning and education. We sat down as a family and discussed whether he would benefit starting his secondary education at a boarding school.

'There will be fewer people in a class so you will get more attention and there are teachers who will be on hand to help you with your homework at night,' I reasoned. Michael agreed it was for the best and Declan said he would give it a go. I think he wanted help as much as we wanted it for him.

We sent him away to Gordonstoun, way up past Inverness. It was where Prince Charles went to school. We chose it because it was in Scotland and I thought it would be easy to drive to. I always used to say that I didn't understand people who had children and then sent them away to boarding school. Now I was doing it myself. But I was doing it because he needed it.

'Why didn't you just give up work and look after him?' some of my friends said to me. I didn't know how to educate Declan because I was no good at that sort of thing. I left school at 15 with no qualifications. I wanted the best for my boy and my kids' well-being came first.

We took him up to school for his first term and, when the moment to say goodbye finally arrived, I think I was a lot more anxious than I thought I'd be. Yes, okay, I'd spent many nights away from my kids on business but we had never been apart for longer than a week. I was going to be separated from my boy for weeks at a time. My mothering instinct kicked in. Declan was given a dorm room and I panicked. 'This is too small for him,' I turned to Michael. 'It's not laid out properly. I'm not comfortable with him being in this room,' I fussed.

'*Muuuum*,' Declan pleaded.

'No, Declan, just listen to your mother,' I pushed.

I had him moved to another dorm but I had a few more adjustments still to make.

'Right, Declan, stay out. I'm going to put up your posters, I'm going to sort out your desk,' I insisted. Declan rolled his eyes but both he and Michael knew me too well and let me get on with organising. I sorted all his pencils out, I hung up all of his posters and I made his bed. I brought Declan back in and told him what was what.

'That is where your socks go,' I said. 'That is where your boxer shorts go. These are the hangers you use for those shirts.'

'Right, okay, Mum,' he said. He was used to it.

'And that's your bag for your dirty laundry and these are where your towels go and dirty ones, you hang them up over there,' I pointed to the hooks. I kind of trained him up, there in the room. I couldn't leave until I knew that he got it.

'Socks go in there, towels go up there,' he recited.

'And you can call me any time,' I fussed.

'*Yeeeees*, Mum,' Declan said and fell back on his bed.

It broke my heart when we left. I am so close to my kids and it was times like that when I realised quite how much I loved them and how I needed them as much as they needed me. I felt like it was another emotional journey and I bit my lip to stop myself crying in the car. I hated being away from Declan. I hated not being able to kiss him goodnight. So much so that I would drive the six-hour round trip every week so I could see him.

The housemaster eventually told me I had to stop. 'You need to leave him alone to settle in,' he said.

I was now the one being told off! I had also been phoning him three times a day and I was told to stop that as well. I suppose I was just really lonely without all my children around me. But

I didn't want my feelings to affect Declan, so I did what I was told. But I've never been ambitious for my children. I've never been that pushy mum. I want my kids to decide for themselves what will make them happy. I really don't mind what they do with their lives as long as they are happy.

19

OBE

*When you choose to forgive those who
have hurt you, you take away their power.*

'Do you want to come and watch this show I'm starring in tonight?' Mel B from the Spice Girls asked. When I found out it was a naked peep show with her on stage alongside a bunch of other naked girls, I thought Jesus Christ! I'm not going to that thing, no way.

'No, thanks, I'm all right,' I declined. I'm actually quite prudish when it comes to those sorts of things. I don't like getting undressed in front of people. When I was growing up, if anyone was kissing on the TV, my dad would shout: 'Get that off' to my mum.

Mel B was our first black model when we signed her in 2008. My brand is for all types of women and I wanted to show we were not just for blondes. I also go for people with personality and she had bags of that. We got her when we were shooting our autumn/winter 2009 brochure in Las Vegas in the USA.

It wasn't a straightforward set-up. I got wound up because we couldn't get a licence to shoot outside. We couldn't shoot in the famous Bellagio hotel either and then we could shoot in the Bellagio and then Mel B turned up all hyped from the evening before.

She told me all about the beautiful women she had been dancing with. I think she lived up to her Spice Girl name of Scary Spice at that point. She did scare me a wee bit because she was just going on about the show a little too much.

It was a stressful start but it actually turned out to be amazing with the pictures we got in the nightclub. Mel B is a true professional and one of my hardest-working models. Some models say they have had enough after six underwear changes but Mel got up to something like 40 changes – she was a grafter and so down to earth. You would think that for someone who used to be in the Spice Girls, one of the biggest girl bands in the world, she would be a diva, but she so wasn't. She put the hours in, she worked hard on her body too and she looked incredible in a red satin corset and thong. We finished and celebrated our hard work by going for some drinks and watching the famous fountain and firework show.

'Can I have a double vodka, please?' I asked the waiter. I'd been so stressed – I needed a release. 'Thank god for that,' I said, raising my glass. I knocked them back, one after the other. Shot after shot after shot. What I didn't realise was that the vodka shots in Vegas were double what they were in the UK. I didn't drink at the best of times, let alone double measures. I'd been drinking close to four shots per glass!

After hardly any time, the view of the fountains started to spin. My eyes rolled into my head. I felt like I was going to pass out. I turned to Michael for help because we had to walk through miles of hotel before we got to our room. The Bellagio was massive and full of betting tables and fruit machines. It felt like it went on for miles.

'Michael, please take me to my room,' I slurred.

He looked at me and shook his head. 'I'm not walking all the way back, go yourself,' he said.

My head was spinning at a hundred miles an hour now. 'Please, please take me,' I begged. I wasn't used to feeling drunk. 'I can't go on my own. I feel as if I'm going to collapse.'

Michael got really cross. 'You're nothing but a pain in the arse,' he grumbled, as he hooked his arm through mine.

I was bouncing off the fruit machines like a pinball as Michael walked me to our room. 'Please stay with me,' I begged Michael as he plonked me on the bed. I was so scared because I hadn't ever been that drunk before. *What's happened to me? Has my drink been spiked?* Of course, it was just the bloody vodka and the fact that I'd been necking quadruple shots of it, but I didn't realise that at the time.

'You are not ruining my night. Just get into bed,' he moaned.

'Please, I don't want to be on my own, please help me,' I whimpered.

'Just throw up and go to your bed,' he said.

Michael left me to it, and I stumbled into the bathroom to see if I could make myself sick. But I couldn't throw up so I fell back instead.

I remember lying like a starfish on the warm tiles of the bathroom. The room was spinning. I started to feel even worse. So what did I do? I decided to run a bath. I thought a cool dip would help me. I tried to make myself sick again but I couldn't throw up. I couldn't get it to come up. I slithered into the bath and I don't remember what happened next but I must have sunk like a block of lead.

I woke up under the water, choking. I tried to pull myself out but my hands slipped. *Splash.* I slipped back under. 'Help,' I spluttered. I kept sinking under the water. I was choking and coughing. I thought I was going to die. I finally managed to get a grip on the handles and pulled myself so I was half hanging over the side. It was a frightening experience. I almost drowned in the bath.

I was still drunk but my heart was racing. I felt like it was going to jump out of my chest. I clambered out and crawled to the toilet where I was finally sick.

I felt my way to my mobile and called Michael. 'I've almost drowned in the bath. Please come and get me,' I cried.

'I'll get you when I'm ready to come back,' he said. I fell asleep on the tiles in the bathroom after that and woke up with a whopping hangover.

I appeared on the Ultimo brochures for 2009 with Mel B. I had lost five stone in total and I was looking and feeling good. That year was also memorable because we launched our first range for younger girls, Miss Ultimo. It was to be funky, edgy, trendy and completely different to the look of Ultimo. It was a new brand with a completely new DNA that would not compete with Ultimo. I've always made sure that all the brands I've invented don't compete with one another, be they Ultimo, Miss Ultimo, Ultimo swimwear, Ultimo shapewear, Michelle for George, Bra Queen Michelle, Michelle Innovations for Dunnes stores or Adore Moi for Debenhams.

Miss Ultimo was aimed at 14- to 18-year-olds and I wanted someone cool to launch and be the face of the new line. Peaches Geldof immediately popped into my head. Peaches had a lot of tattoos, including a daisy chain that ran from her knee to her chest. Personally, I don't agree with tattoos. I don't have one myself but I still thought that she was the coolest young girl about town. She was always being photographed out and about in London and I think a lot of girls her age liked her style. I wanted her for my brand.

I met Peaches at her manager's office in London and I was completely blown away by her. She was a writer for a New York magazine and she was so intelligent. The conversations we used to have together were nothing like those I'd had with my other models – Peaches loved debating. She was quite something and very mature for her age, being only 20 at the time. We got on exceptionally well. Peaches respected where I'd come from and how I'd built my business up from nothing and I respected that she wasn't just a daft little lassie. She was different from all the other teenagers I knew.

Her vulnerability came through on our first shoot. She clung on to her hair and make-up team, constantly asking for reassurance. 'Are you sure I should wear it like that?' she asked repeatedly. But I think anyone that age is vulnerable. I felt vulnerable at 20. You don't really know who you are yet.

We did the shoot in a bowling alley to complement the edgy, fun look we were going for. She was very nervous to start with, not surprisingly as it was her first lingerie shoot. After the first hour behind the camera she relaxed. We signed her for a year, with an option to extend, and we launched Miss Ultimo in May 2009. It was a very successful campaign – the brand was hot.

Peaches' pictures appeared in trendy magazines that Ultimo would never get into.

I had something to celebrate myself not long after that. It was autumn 2009 and my PA got a call from Buckingham Palace. She came running across the office at rocket speed to speak to me. 'What is it?' I said, concerned.

'There's a woman from Buckingham Palace on the phone about an OBE for you,' she panted, out of breath. 'They say they've given it to you, but apparently you don't want it,' she went on.

'What?' She had my attention now. 'Shut the fuck up!' I spluttered. I burst out laughing. 'They are having a laugh, this is a radio show doing a wind-up.' I dismissed the call. 'Look, there is no way I've got an OBE. Go tell the woman that we'll phone her back because we don't believe it's true.'

I got back to work while my PA passed on my message. A few minutes later, she was back with the phone number for Buckingham Palace. 'Okay, I'll ring it,' I sighed. Curiosity got the better of me. It bloody well was Buckingham Palace and I had been awarded an OBE. I nearly dropped the phone in shock. 'We assumed you didn't want to accept your OBE as we hadn't heard anything back,' said the very well-spoken lady. Apparently, they sent the invitation to my old house.

'I haven't been living at that address for several years,' I explained. 'I... I... I don't know what to say.'

'Well, do you want to accept it?' she asked.

'Oh, my god, of course I want to accept it,' I screamed. It was a dream come true.

'Thanks so much, tell the Queen I'm over the moon, ' I said.

I had to keep the award a secret until it was announced in

the 2010 New Year's Honours list. You can imagine it was really hard. I told my family straight away. 'What, say that again?' Mum and Dad said when I broke the news. They couldn't believe what they were hearing. Their daughter had been awarded one of the highest honours in the UK. 'Oh, my god, who would have ever thought?' Mum squealed.

I was over the moon. It was amazing they gave it to me but there were many other people who had helped me. My family and all my team at Ultimo had worked so hard. Above all, it was proof that it is possible to achieve your dreams no matter where you are from. I wanted my OBE to be an inspiration for kids growing up. If I can do it, they can do it too.

The next thing I had to think about was – what was I going to wear? Well, I've been given it for the business that I'm in, so I should wear something that represents Ultimo. I know, I'll design a corset, I thought. A very sophisticated, outerwear corset, mind. I wouldn't dream of meeting the Queen in my underwear!

So I turned my hand to designing this beautiful black creation which had a lace detail at the top and panels that ran down the side to emphasise my curves. I also made a hat, delicately woven in leopard print – it had a wide brim and I finished it off with a scattering of pheasant feathers. It was beautiful. I complemented the outfit with fitted black trousers, a floor-length black velvet coat and, of course, black Louboutin heels. I had fun choosing the outfits for the kids and I helped Michael pick a suit.

We all travelled down to London together and I remember it being bitterly cold when we arrived at Buckingham Palace. We were ushered into one of the grand halls, which had gold-painted walls and a red carpet. I had butterflies as I watched everyone go up in turn to get their OBEs and MBEs. It was such a humbling moment to be around all these incredible people who had contributed so much in one way or another.

They called my name and my heart leapt out of my chest. I gave my kids a huge grin as I stood up and made my way down the red carpet to be handed my medal by Princess Anne. It didn't seem real. I'd launched Ultimo in Selfridges just over ten years ago and now I was being honoured for my contribution to business, being one of the three most successful female entrepreneurs in the country and creating a company worth multi-millions and achieving over a billion pounds worth of press coverage.

I walked out of the Palace into a sea of press and photographers. 'Michelle, just one more,' the paps called out. 'Over here, Michelle.' The press wanted to interview me and take pictures of me holding the OBE before we could do the official family photo.

'That's it. We are not waiting any longer,' Michael ordered. He said the kids were freezing and he'd had enough.

'Hang on, I want an official picture with me and the kids and you,' I pleaded.

The press photos were just a formality. The family picture meant the most to me, something I would be able keep on my mantelpiece forever.

'No, let's go,' Michael said and walked off.

I was heartbroken. I'd never be able to get that moment back. We went on to Scott's restaurant in Mayfair, one of my favourite restaurants, where Michael and I proceeded to have a massive row.

It was supposed to be this amazing celebration. I'd planned it to be the perfect day, but it was so not. We were sitting in this fancy restaurant but everyone was in a mood. Michael and I weren't speaking and the kids were grumpy, thinking, Why are we here? Don't get me wrong – receiving the OBE was incredible – but I went back to Glasgow, took my hat off and thought, I don't know why I bothered. I swept my disappointment under the carpet as I had done so many times before and got on with doing what I'd been given an OBE for.

We'd done a second shoot with Peaches in a fairground but not long after those pictures came out, Peaches appeared in a different sort of photo shoot. I picked up the *News of the World* on a Sunday in March 2010 and said, 'Jesus Christ!' Splattered across the paper were topless pictures of Peaches with a large plaster covering her thigh, taken by some guy who claimed to have had a heroin-fuelled, one-night stand with her in the previous November.

I called an emergency meeting. 'What are we going to do? This is a nightmare,' I started. Peaches was promoting our brand to teenagers who looked up to her. To see her with needle marks everywhere wasn't good for her image. 'Why is she doing this?' I shook my head in sadness. It was tragic. It was also very much out of the blue because I'd never sensed Peaches was into that kind of stuff and I hadn't seen any marks on her body during our shoots.

At our directors' meeting the next morning we discussed the number of emails from unhappy customers as a result of the story. The emails were saying things like, 'You have a responsibility, Michelle, to get shot of this girl' and 'I don't want my daughter looking at her thinking this behaviour is acceptable.'

And then came the emails from the big buyers who were

taking Peaches' pictures out of the stores. 'We want to know what your position is,' they demanded. I dropped my head into my hands. I felt under incredible pressure as well as deeply sorry for Peaches. Being a mum myself I felt so concerned for her future. When someone is down you should never boot them in the face. I'd been kicked many times by the press and I knew what it was like. I felt really, really bad but I had no choice but to terminate her contract.

I sent a letter to Peaches and to her management as well, saying: 'I wish you all the best, but I have to do this, being a founder of this brand. I hope everything is fine and that we could remain friends.'

Her management were so nice with their response. They said: 'Michelle, we understand and we really appreciate what you've done for Peaches.'

The media like to exaggerate things and say I sacked her but that wasn't the case. There was no fall out – I was really concerned and worried about her. But at the end of the day I had to protect the brand and say that needle marks are not acceptable and heroin use is not acceptable because we have a responsibility to teenagers. The whole thing was deeply sad.

20

TAKING THE PLUNGE

Believe in yourself. Just believe.

The whole episode with Peaches came at a pivotal moment in my life. I'd been asked to star in a new TV show called *71 Degrees North*, which follows ten celebrities as they try to make it to the North Cape, Norway, at 71 degrees north of the equator. None of the other TV work I'd done was anything like this. I'd starred in *Celebrity Apprentice* for Comic Relief but this was something else. This was going to be a month living in a tent in Arctic conditions.

I couldn't believe they were asking me. *Me* – who has blow-dries three times a week and is used to all the luxury and comforts of a millionaire lifestyle. Why not me? I thought. I'd been to hell and back in nearly losing the company and nothing could ever be as bad as that. Walking through a bit of snow certainly wouldn't come close, so what did I have to fear? Plus now I'd lost just over five stone, I had a chance to get fit with it.

I told my mum I'd be living in a tent for a month, without washing my hair, without restaurants, wearing no make-up (because it would freeze) and – most importantly – no Blackberry. She said, 'I'll help you pack your bags.' Her response followed on from the chat I'd had with my parents about turning into a diva. Mum thought that the challenge would be the perfect way to help me remember who I really was and get back to the Michelle they once knew and loved before I had the big house and the five cars. 'That's what you need,' she said.

I got serious cold feet when the time came for me to leave. Firstly, I was nervous about leaving my kids – I was worried I'd really miss them. And I was worried about not having my Blackberry. As I packed my bags I thought, Am I doing the right thing here? Am I going to cope with this?

But I did need a break, from everything – work, Michael and fighting with Michael. I'd left school at 15 and all my friends had gone on holidays, partying in Spain and Ibiza, but I'd never had that. I was pregnant at 19 and I'd worked every day God sent since I was 15. I'd never had an actual break away from the kids and the business. I'd never done anything for *me*. I was excited to find out about me, because I didn't really know who I was any more. I'd lost my way a bit.

I remember meeting everyone at the airport at Gatwick and thinking, Oh, God, that Joe Absolom from *EastEnders*, I'm going to really fight with him. He's just rude. Susie Amy from *Footballers' Wives* was there and I thought she was beautiful. Gavin Henson, I thought, He loves himself. Shane Richie was also starring in the show and my first impression was that he seemed like the same guy you see on the TV. I had these preconceived ideas but it didn't turn out that way at all. We became close because we were all stuck in the middle of nowhere under extreme weather conditions.

The others actually relied on me a lot to organise things. I was sharing a tent with Shane, Joe and Gavin and it was an absolute mess the first night. Shane Richie's boots were everywhere. Gavin was looking for his socks. 'They're your socks… these are my socks,' said Gavin as he rummaged through the mess.

My OCD took over. I called the boys to attention. 'Enough, guys,' I shouted. 'I am not putting up with this for the next month, so here are the rules.' They all stood to attention like school kids. 'Number one: you do not bring your dirty snow boots into this tent. You leave them outside the door. One beside the other, left boot next to right boot. Because you're bringing them in and soaking all the sleeping bags and it's not fair.

'And you,' I said, pointing to Shane, 'that's your area there. You keep your socks, your goggles and your gloves in the netting there where you sleep. You are not going to leave them all over the floor. You all need to organise your sleeping bags because I don't want to see your sleeping bag on my patch, okay?'

'Yes,' they said in chorus.

'Great,' I said and dusted off my hands.

Four days later they all thanked me. 'This is running like a company,' Shane said.

We were tested to our absolute limits by taking part in challenges like swimming in frozen fjords, kayaking for five hours at a time and jumping into the icy sea. The team who won the challenge got to spend a night in a cosy log cabin while the losers went back to a freezing tent to sleep in minus 25° temperatures. I was completely out of my comfort zone and I was forced to overcome a lot of my fears, such as my phobia of heights.

One of the challenges was to cross a ravine on a web of rope, and I was terrified, absolutely terrified. I also had this heavy rucksack on my back and I thought I was going to topple over at any second. 'I can't do this,' I screamed. My legs had turned to jelly. 'Get me down, get me down.'

I gave up halfway through but then Joe appeared behind me. 'Keep going,' he shouted. He knew I had it in me to fight on.

'I can't,' I cried. The tears froze to my cheek.

'Trust me, you can,' he encouraged me. So I slowly put one foot in front of the other and I kept going until I reached the other side. It was the scariest moment of the whole show for me and also my proudest when I finished.

I had not anticipated how tough it would be and simple things became huge challenges in those conditions, like having to light a fire to boil some snow because I was thirsty in the middle of the night. We were tested in other ways too, such as through Shane Richie's snoring. God, it was unbelievable, it was so loud. Joe and I were next to him and couldn't get a wink of sleep.

Life out there was an emotional rollercoaster. There were some moments when I was freezing and so exhausted that I thought, What the hell am I doing out here? I don't need to be here. I woke up one night with ice all over my eyelashes and I burst into tears. 'That's it. I'm packing up and going home,' I cried to Joe.

'No, you're not,' he shouted and he warmed me up, zipping me into my sleeping bag and telling me to shut it. He was right, of course, and the fighter in me said that giving in went against everything I stood for. When I first met him I thought he was going to be nightmare to get on with, but he was the total opposite. Joe turned out to be one of the most incredible guys.

There were also moments when I found myself reflecting on my life. I realised how spoilt I was and how I didn't need half the things I owned. I had some peace and quiet for the first time ever and thoughts were racing through my head, like, You only live once and why should you be unhappy? Work isn't the be-all and end-all of life. You need money to survive but happiness is more important.

I probably should have used the time to reflect on my marriage and ask myself why I was putting up with so much crap. Why I just didn't leave Michael. But believe it or not, I never actually thought about getting a divorce. Like I said before, I came from a place where you just get on with it, no matter what. I had kids and a business with Michael and I suppose I was very loyal. I know so many couples who are miserable but they'd never leave their partner because of the kids. To be honest though, I didn't really think about Michael that much when I was out there. I was so relaxed and I was getting a lot more mellow and calm and appreciating things.

I thought, Why have I moaned at the Dorchester? It's like living in a fairy tale to stay there. As long as the bed is clean and it's safe and tidy, does it really matter? We were sleeping on top of rocks and snow, which kind of put everything into perspective.

I missed my kids dreadfully though. When it was Mother's Day the producers handed me a box. I opened it up and it was full of cards and presents from all of my kids. Usually they just signed their name but this time the left-hand side of the card was a long message: 'Can't wait until you get home, so proud of you, Mum.'

'Really miss you, Mum.'

'How are you getting on with the heights? Ha, ha, ha.'

'What's it like not having your blow-dry?'

They were funny and sweet and I broke down in tears. I missed them so much. That's when I realised I'd had enough and I wanted to go home. 'Please vote for me. I want to go home now, I've had my time,' I said to all the guys when it came to voting to send someone home. I'm still friendly with all of them to this day. The whole experience changed my life – and for the better. I decided I'd work to live rather than live to work. I started to question if I still wanted to run a business in the next few years and let it take over my life. I decided I would learn to put my Blackberry down. I was addicted to my phone before. I used to sleep with it under my pillow. I'd say I came out of there a much nicer person. Business is like a train that you can't get off and I think I finally got off.

I came home on a high. But no sooner had I landed than the press began to make out that I was having an affair with one of the guys on the show. We'd organised a night out for everyone to laugh about our crazy adventure. We met in the Dorchester bar in London for a quick drink before heading out to a restaurant. Michael popped in to say 'Hello' and meet the cast. He left to meet one of his friends and the rest of us went shortly after to have some food. I was wearing really uncomfortable shoes and teetering along the pavement at a snail's pace. Shane Richie turned around and said, 'Come on, you Scottish pain in the arse.' He grabbed my arm to help me along.

We had a really fun evening at a Hix restaurant. I got home before midnight with no idea about the storm that was brewing. I woke up on 16 April 2010 to see that pictures of Shane and I were plastered all over the papers with 'rumours of an affair'.

My heart sank. Of course, it wasn't bloody true. We were all together in a group but the paparazzi, who were stalking us, honed in on me and Shane linking arms and cut out everyone around us. I knew what was coming. Michael used that to absolutely hammer me.

'Michael, why are you doing this?' I pleaded. 'You were with us ten minutes before at the Dorchester and then we all went out as a group after you left. You know there is nothing going on.'

But he was like a bull in a china shop. '*My* wife has been seen grabbing the arm of a guy,' he yelled.

'I was just grabbing his arm in a friendly way because I was crossing the road to catch up with everyone else who were a few paces in front of us and my new shoes were killing my feet and I came back at 11.30 pm and they dropped me home,' I explained in one breath.

There was no reasoning with Michael. 'It's fucking embarrassing. I can't believe my wife grabbing someone else's arm,' he went on. He really laid into me – it was so bad. 'I'm the talk of the town. Everyone thinks I'm such an idiot.' Michael turned and glared. 'How dare you make a fool of me?'

I burst into tears. 'I didn't do anything wrong,' I sobbed.

I would never cheat on my husband; it wasn't in my make-up. I felt so beaten down that I went underground for a few days. I then released a statement to the press to try and calm the situation for the sake of my family and Shane's. 'Last week was tough. All I would like to say, in order to end rumours, is Shane Richie and I are friends but nothing else. When you live in the Arctic in a tent at minus 35 in extreme conditions you all become close! When the TV show starts, it will become clear. I am sorry I put my family through all this last week.'

I hadn't thought much about my marriage while I was away in the Arctic, but since I'd come back, it was all I could think about – how I was trapped in a loveless relationship. How the marriage was basically over.

I wanted to believe that Michael would love me again if I lost the weight. It couldn't have been further from reality. The thinner I got, the bigger my profile grew and the more attention I received, the nastier Michael became. I think he was jealous of all the attention I was getting. He showed it through all the arguments and his total lack of respect for me. I suppose the fact I was earning four times more than Michael, thanks to my speeches and TV work, may have had a part to play. Michael had been the breadwinner when we married, and now the roles had been reversed. To add to that, the spotlight was always on me. Perhaps he felt emasculated?

The good thing was that losing the weight and starring in *71 Degrees North* had given me such a boost in confidence that his words didn't have such an impact on me any more. I felt like I wasn't depressed. I was really starting to get my life on track. Yes, I wasn't in a happy marriage, but I was starting to feel like a woman again. I was starting to feel sexy again.

I remember stepping on the scales one morning, and screaming with happiness because I'd lost the last couple of pounds I'd wanted to shift. I'd gone from 17 and a half stone to 11 and a half stone, I'd dropped from a size 22 to a size 12. I couldn't bloody believe it. 'Michelle, you did it,' I told my reflection in the bathroom cabinet.

It reminded me about a promise I'd made on a beach nearly five years ago. I pulled out my notebook and I read the promise I'd made to Rachel Hunter that I needed to do a photo shoot one day to encourage real women that they too can lose weight. I was to be an inspiration for all those unhappy women out there.

A tear ran down my cheek and splashed onto the page. It was such an emotional moment for me. I thought, I've worked so hard for this. I had given my all to my family but this was for me. I felt it was something I needed to do to get closure. And what's more, I never wrote down a goal without achieving it. It was still there, still on the page, waiting for me to tick it off.

I spoke to Michael. 'I really want to do this, please,' I pleaded.

'No way are you going to do a shoot,' he said.

'Michael, it's not as if we sell tyres. We sell lingerie. I believe in the product and I want to tell people, I want to tell the world I believe in what I sell. I want to encourage women to lose weight by showing it is possible. I am living proof it's possible to change.'

You know, I couldn't even wear my underwear at one point because my arse was too fat. Ultimo goes up to a size 18 and I could wear the bras but I couldn't wear the pants. I had to buy the pants from Marks & Spencer.

'Over my dead body,' Michael said. 'My wife is not going to model our bras.'

'But it's our company,' I pleaded.

'I don't care. You're not doing it,' he said and walked off.

Why couldn't he understand? Why couldn't he just support me? Sod him. I'll do the photo shoot anyway and then when I show him the pictures, he'll change his mind.

I called Dan, who had been a friend and photographer for Ultimo for years, and sneakily arranged a photo shoot without

Michael knowing. We did it in the May Fair, a beautiful five-star hotel in London. I flew down the day before, and I was calm until it came to bedtime. I lay awake for hours, turning everything over in my head. I could hear Michael's words, 'Over my dead body'. I could hear my own voice, doubting whether I could appear on the other side of the camera. Somewhere, I still felt like a fat person in a thin body.

Dan Kennedy turned up at the hotel the next morning and I freaked out. 'I can't do this,' I said, shaking my head in fear.

'Why?' he flashed his cheeky grin.

I broke down in tears. 'I just can't do it, Dan,' I sobbed. 'Michael doesn't know I'm here. He'd kill me if he knew I was here. I hate lying.'

Dan gave me a cuddle and told me to take my time. 'What do you want to do?' he asked.

'I really really want to do it, but I don't know if I can do it,' I explained. I was stuck between a rock and a hard place.

'Well, if it's always been your goal, you should do it,' Dan said. He knew I had the fighter inside me.

I nodded my head and wiped my tears. It was 9.30 am and I ordered a bottle of wine. I sat in my dressing gown, in the suite, drinking wine, as the hair and make-up team worked their magic. The same talented team that had worked with Rachel, Sarah and Mel B were now working on *me*, transforming me, with a completely different look, into a model. They added hair extensions that tumbled halfway down my back. They coloured my eyes to look smoky and sexy and swept bronzer across my face to give me a healthy glow. They finished off my look with a slick of nude lip gloss.

Everything was beautiful; I'd changed my image completely.

I'd never been done up like that before. I felt like a movie star. I put on the lingerie and I couldn't believe how much weight I'd lost. It moulded to my figure perfectly. I'd designed all the pieces as one-offs for the shoot. They weren't for a collection – they were just for me, to show off my transformation. I'd even designed a bow of black feathers on one of the black bras. I felt amazing. I wanted to cry but I bit my lip because I didn't want my mascara to run!

I'd almost drunk the whole bottle of wine by the time I emerged from the bathroom. I had my dressing gown on and Dan turned to me. 'Right, I'm ready,' he announced. I looked at all the photo equipment and my heart raced. I was so nervous. There was no way I could do this in front of everyone.

'Could you all please leave? I have to do this alone,' I said. They all wished me luck while I was shaking.

Dan came up to me and said, 'Okay, take it off.' He pointed to the dressing gown.

'I… I can't,' I said, clinging to it.

'Take it off,' he said.

'No, I can't,' I said.

'Yes, you can, take it off,' he said.

So I took it off. I was shaking like a leaf and the first few pictures were awful. After about half an hour, I got into the swing of it. I remembered all the things I'd learnt in the years of directing our photo shoots – how to pose, how to not to hold your hands like a fan. I think the wine might have helped a bit too!

I left the shoot thinking, Yee hah! I did it. I decided on the plane home that I wanted to find 20 women, real women, and transform them for a photo shoot to make them feel as incredible as I had felt today. I pulled out my notebook and started making a plan for our next campaign.

I came back with all the pictures and showed them to Michael, smiling, 'I'm sorry, but I wanted to do it. What do you think?' I wanted him to tell me how beautiful I looked after all those years of calling me names. These pictures were so classy and tasteful.

Instead, Michael shouted at me and he threw the pictures across the room. 'You are not releasing those pictures. You put them in your top drawer and never bring them out again,' he ordered.

'No, Michael, I've worked for years to get to this.'

He went around all of our friends, telling them how I had betrayed him; how he couldn't believe I'd done it behind his back.

All I was doing was celebrating saying goodbye to all of the years of trauma, the years of heartache, the years of being miserable and the years of being depressed. I just felt that by finally ticking the big box of doing this shoot I had changed my life.

You will not speak to me like that.

'I am proud of these images and I want to encourage women to do the same,' I stood my ground. But my words fell on deaf ears.

'You will ruin this business. There is no other businesswoman who strips for their brand,' he blasted.

I threw my arms up in despair. 'This is the business I love. These are the bras that I started designing ten years ago. This is the brand I started and I love this business. I'm doing it for me, I'm doing it for the business and I'm going to release these pictures,' I told him.

So fuck you.

'No, you will not,' he said, shaking his head like I was bluffing.

'You want a bet?' I put my hands on my hips. 'You watch this space.' It was my turn to turn and walk out.

The next day I chose nine of the best photos. My favourite was a shot of me standing at the end of the bed. I didn't look slutty in them and it wasn't as if I was wearing see-through underwear showing my nipples. You'd show more flesh in a bikini on the beach than I did in that hotel room. I told my PR girl, Claire, to release the pictures.

'I can't,' she protested. 'I'll lose my job. He's threatened to sack me if I do.'

'Claire, I've worked so hard to get to this. I want you to release them,' I ordered.

I released the pictures on 26 October 2010. I wasn't going to be controlled or bullied any more.

21

CARING AND SHARING

There are two types of pain in this world:
pain that hurts you and pain that changes you.

I had organised my own photo shoot and the pictures went everywhere.

MICHELLE MONE HIRES HERSELF AS AN UNDERWEAR MODEL AFTER LOSING SIX STONE, was just one of the many headlines splashed across the papers all around the world. The best thing was that the press were so complimentary and so supportive. It was such a relief because it could have gone the other way. They could have asked, 'What the hell does she think she's doing? She's a businesswoman not a model.'

I've always been a risk-taker and this one paid off. I've taken a lot of inspiration from Richard Branson – he does things for his brand all the time. I love my brand and I don't mind if the world sees me in it. I felt confident wearing my own underwear for the very first time in my life and I wanted to shout from the rooftops, 'I'm not fat any more.' I was like a wilted flower that had grown again.

I received an incredible 17,000 letters of support from the public. There was only one bad one out of all of those. I've kept them all and I haven't forgotten about them. If I ever feel a bit low or in need of a confidence boost I pull out the letters to remind myself of what I've achieved. 'Good for you, Michelle. You've really inspired me and you've really encouraged me,' were just some of the many words of support.

One letter that really moved me came from a woman who, just like me, had no confidence. She described how sad and lonely she'd felt but how I had finally given her the courage to lose the weight. I can't tell you how emotional I felt reading these letters from women who had been through everything that I had suffered.

Those pictures of me did wonders for the brand, but I'd say they were the nail in the coffin for my marriage. Things just got worse and worse after that. I did an interview in which the journalist asked me, 'Was your husband proud of you for doing this?' I was standing at a crossroads. Do I tell the truth or do I pretend everything is okay?

'No, actually, he didn't want me to do it,' I admitted. *I'm not going to lie. Why should I?* I was proud of those pictures and Michael had tried to stop me helping other women do the same. 'He was appalled I'd posed in my underwear. He didn't speak to me for days,' I said.

Michael went mental when he read the headlines. 'Why did you tell the press that?' he shouted.

'Because that's the truth,' I shrugged. 'And don't think that I'm going to lie for you.' I'd had enough. The worm had turned.

I threw myself into thinking of ways I could help more people. I'd got a huge rush from all the women telling me I'd given them courage and confidence to change their lives and I was thinking, What next? Who can I help next? I suppose it also went back to *71 Degrees North* and those feelings I had had when I was sleeping in a freezing tent on just rock and snow. I'd decided then that I was going to give more to my family and to those who needed my help.

I launched the Ultimo Real Women search. I wanted to find 20 women whose confidence I could help to boost with a makeover and a photo shoot. I felt it was my duty to showcase women of all shapes and sizes and make them feel good about themselves. I wasn't necessarily looking for sad stories, but I did hear some moving accounts from some of the women we discovered. One woman had breast cancer. Another women had been bullied for being fat. They were real stories that so many women could relate to.

One story in particular sticks with me to this day. It was a woman whose husband walked out on her and the kids. She was 46 and had no confidence whatsoever but she met someone four weeks after appearing in the Real Women campaign and she's now remarried and happy.

I'd always been caring but I started to care a lot more after the campaign and I had money to help others. One morning I was listening to the radio as I was making breakfast for the kids. Michael was in the kitchen when the 7.30 am news came on. There was an appeal for a girl who desperately needed help. The poor lassie was only 24 and dying of leukaemia. She'd gone away with her friends on a snowboarding holiday but hadn't bothered with travel insurance because she thought there was no point with her terminal illness. She went on to have this really bad accident and was now in a coma. Her family needed £20,000 to bring her home and they were pleading for people to ring in with donations. It was heartbreaking.

I turned to Michael as I was buttering the kids' toast. 'I want to bring her home,' I said.

He looked up at me. 'Okay lets do it,' he nodded. For that brief moment we put our differences aside. I phoned the radio station and they were really shocked. I told them not to mention my name because I didn't want it to be a publicity thing. I didn't want it to be about me. I just wanted to get this girl home. Giving that money made me feel much better than the feeling I got when I bought a flashy car.

Whoosh, a rocket had taken off inside me. There was no stopping me now. I was on a path to helping others and at the same time helping myself grow stronger. It sounds cheesy but I was like titanium – nothing could touch me. I stood up for myself in every way imaginable and my confidence led to constant fighting in the office with Michael. Some of those arguments were disgusting. Our weekly boardroom meetings couldn't go on for longer than 15 minutes because we would explode. He'd walk out or I'd walk out and going into work became similar to walking through a minefield.

I began to associate a bad feeling with our new office in East Kilbride because of all the fighting that was going on. That office didn't feel right. It had never felt right, if I'm honest. It was too big and too segregated – too show homey. Just like the house I'd built, it was the biggest and the best but it was where I was at my most unhappy. I would go from one show home to the other. From one battleground in the day to another in the evening. Michael would go to bed and turn the other way and I would do the same. There was a cold front between us, with most of the arguments taking place in the office. We tried to keep our fighting away from the kids as much as possible.

Looking back now, I really don't know how I put up with it for so long. I guess a lot of people reading this might be asking why I didn't just leave and why I didn't get a divorce. I suppose the simple answer is that I never give up. I keep fighting. It's all I've ever known and I thought, If I keep fighting, somehow everything might turn out okay in the end.

It soon became clear that Michael had a different approach. It must have been around summer 2011 when I hired Samantha Bunn as head of design. She had previously worked for us and I'd been trying to get her back ever since she left a year and a half earlier. I suppose I took her under my wing. I spent a lot of time training her up. We got on well so I said she could stay in our guesthouse next door to our place. Sam, who was 31 at the time, confided in me about her boyfriend troubles, how he wouldn't ask her to marry her. 'Don't worry. You won't be on your own,' I reassured her that we were only next door if she needed us. I felt sorry for Sam, so I invited her for dinner with my family on some nights. Michael would do the cooking and we'd all sit around the kitchen table, chatting and laughing.

I let her stay with me when we went on business trips to London. I gave her the spare room at my new flat in Mayfair and we would sometimes stay up talking about her relationship problems. I treated Sam like a family friend. I trusted her. I thought everything was hunky-dory and then all of a sudden, Sam started pushing the boundaries. She would pop around for dinner with Michael and the kids while I was away in London on business.

That's just stepping over the line. If I invite you into my house then come, but don't just turn up for your dinner when I'm not there. I felt like she was weaving her way into my territory and my hair started to stand up on end. It wasn't long before I sensed something was going on between her and Michael. She was always chatting to him in his office with the door shut. There was no reason for her to be there when she was my designer.

I used to catch her in there all the time, flirting and flicking her long dark hair. I spotted what was happening immediately – I've got eyes in the back of my head.

I went in one day and confronted her. 'Why are you here?' I demanded.

His face went bright red and she spluttered a load of rubbish. The pair of them had 'Guilty' written all over their faces. Sam scurried away and I turned to Michael. 'Why is she in your office?'

'Because she's asking me about fabrics,' he said.

'Fabrics? That's got nothing to do with you. You don't manage her, why is she always in your office? And what's more, why are you always closing the door when you leave it open with other staff?' I went on. No answer. 'Are you having an affair with her?'

Michael stood up behind his desk. 'You need to be sectioned,' he shouted.

A few days would pass and then there was something else. It kept happening. There was always another red flag waving in my face. There was one night where Michael took a bottle of red out of the wine rack. 'Where are you going with that? I asked.

'Sam's just texted me. She's got no wine. I'm just going to deliver this to her next door,' he said.

That is so out of character, I thought. He would never normally do that. 'Okay,' I said, shrugging. Fifteen minutes passed and he was still not back. I started to pace up and down the kitchen. Thirty minutes later: still no sign of Michael. My heart raced with anxiety. Something was up. Michael came home an hour later. 'What took you so long?' I demanded.

'We were just talking,' he said.

For an hour? 'What were you talking about?' I said.

'Ah, she was just upset with a few things.'

I was constantly asking Michael if he was having an affair and his answer was always the same – 'You need to be sectioned' or 'You're nuts'. Michael told everyone, even my mum and dad, that I was going mad. 'You're dreaming up all these things.'

He told my mum and my best friend Ilene that I needed to see a doctor and that I needed medication. I started to think, Maybe I am mad? If someone keeps telling you that you're crazy it's hard not to believe it. It had the same effect as him calling me fat over the years. I started to believe I was this big, ugly monster. 'No, Michelle, snap out of it,' I shouted. The writing was on the wall. I wanted to flush him out so I told my friends he was having an affair – I told Ilene, my mum and dad, my PA and my head of finance. I said to everyone that the signs were there.

'They are having an affair,' I swore to Ilene.

'Michael? I don't think so. What makes you think that?' she said.

'Because they are, because she's flirting with him constantly and he's different…' I broke down. 'He's different with me,' I sobbed.

The problem was, I had no concrete proof. There were 101 signs and my gut was telling me – that same intuition I used to suss out people growing up in the East End. I became a woman possessed. I had to know to put my mind at ease. Our arguments became so bad that Michael kicked me out of our bedroom. 'Get out. This is my room,' he said.

I grabbed my pillow and moved to the spare room. Maybe it was for the best because I couldn't lie next to him, imagining what he was getting up to behind my back. I felt sick to the pit of my stomach. I felt so lonely and I remember pouring my heart out one night to Carol Vorderman. We'd been good friends since starring in *Celebrity Apprentice* together and I often gave her my flat in London if she needed somewhere to stay.

We were both in our jammies, curled up on my couch with a glass of wine when I started crying. I'd been confiding in Carol for a while that I thought Michael was having an affair but it had all become a bit too much. I was distraught. 'He wants to get me sectioned,' I cried. 'How can he say that to me?' I shook my head in despair. Carol was really worried about me. She gave me a big hug and tried to calm me down. I had explained to her how it was all just so hurtful. Yes, I'd been unhappy for a long time and, yes, the unhappiness was my fault for staying with him but that was no excuse for what I thought was betrayal. It was a really low blow to be having an affair with *my* designer, in *my* guesthouse.

'My friends are starting to question me; my kids think I'm a nutcase. Even my mum and dad are saying, "There is something not right about our daughter."'

'You need to put your mind at rest,' Carol said. 'If he's telling everyone you're a nutcase and need to be sectioned, you need to find out the truth for yourself.' I started playing around with the idea of hiring a private detective. Carol told me she knew some friends who could put me in touch with someone.

'On second thoughts, that won't be necessary,' I said wiping the tears from my eyes. I guess there was still a part of me that thought we could work things out. I was dreading my 40th on 8th October – I wasn't in the mood at all. How was I going to be able to put on a brave face with everything that was going on? I suppose I'd become an expert in throwing on a smile when I had to perform.

Michael asked me at the last minute, 'What do you want?'

I'd made a massive effort for his 40th. I'd even got Leona Lewis to sing at his party and then I took Michael and all our friends on holiday to Barcelona. 'What do I want? You have to ask me?' I replied. 'Can't you be creative yourself? I was so angry and hurt. I ran through a load of party options in my head and I kept coming back to the place that I felt would help me through this difficult time. Somewhere that gave me strength. 'Michael, I would like nothing fancy,' I started. 'I would like to have my 40th in the place where I grew up. The place that means so much to me. The place that taught me everything.'

I remembered my mum's words: 'Michelle, remember where you came from, who you are.'

'I want my birthday in Coia's Cafe on Duke Street.'

Michael was taken aback. 'Coia's Cafe in the East End? You don't really want to have it there. What's all the press going to think, what are all our friends going to think?'

I stood my ground. I defended my turf. 'I don't care what everyone thinks. I don't care if the press writes, "The bra tycoon has her 40th in a café that sells ice cream, curry sauce and chips." That's where I want it to be,' I said.

I couldn't have wished for a better birthday. All my friends showed up. My mum and dad loved it. My family were thrilled and most of them could get there just by walking across the road. The only person who didn't come was Sam, thank god. The menu was 'Michelle's favourites': curry sauce and chips with pink champagne and pudding was a knickerbocker glory. I wanted to show the people of the East End that I had not forgotten where I was from. Some of them might have thought that just because I was successful I'd turned my back on them. I'll never turn my back on them, never. That's who I am. I'll never pretend to be someone I'm not.

22

CAUGHT RED-HANDED

Stay strong, be positive. We all struggle sometimes.

'Remember, you should never step over the line when it comes to your staff,' I warned Michael at the work Christmas party in 2011. I was so embarrassed. Michael and Sam had been flirting with each other all afternoon. She'd been giggling into his ear and flicking her hair. Michael had been ignoring the rest of the staff. It was a Christmas get-together and we were supposed to be going around the team to give them all a bit of time. He only spent time with Sam. I felt awful. I felt humiliated in front of everyone. I wanted my husband to come home with me at 7 pm and we had a massive argument.

'You should leave now. Let the team get on with it as they can't enjoy themselves as much with us being around,' I insisted. I left on my own. I couldn't sleep until I knew Michael was home. It got later and later and all the while my anxiety levels got higher and higher. I was pretty much pacing the bedroom by the time I eventually heard the taxi pull into the drive and then the two of them giggling. Michael had come home with *her* at 3.30 am.

That was it – that was the final nail in the coffin for me. I'd had enough of this heartache. No one makes a fool of me. I confronted Michael and we had this explosive argument. We barely spoke for the week leading up to Christmas Day. Things were so tense between us. I was still sleeping in the spare room and I was still raging with him but I was determined to make it a good day for the sake of the children.

I pulled Michael aside to make a truce. 'Please, let's make this a good day for the sake of Rebecca, Declan and Bethany,' I pleaded.

Michael agreed that we would talk and get on, which was a massive relief. He got on with making the turkey – he was always the chef of the house. I ran around, cleaning up and making everything look perfect for the kids and the family who were arriving any moment. Michael took the turkey out of the oven to cool down before carving. He then just walked out of the house – walked out on us on Christmas Day.

'Michael,' I screamed after him.

'Dad, Dad, where are you going?' all the kids were crying. He just got in his Porsche and left. I burst into tears. I didn't have any words left. It was truly awful. I was crying and the kids were crying. It took me back to the heartache and tears when I was growing up and we spent Christmas in hospital by my dad's bedside.

My mum and dad arrived in the sea of tears. It felt like someone had died. 'Michelle, what's happened?' my mum said, trying to get some sense out of me.

'He's left us,' I sobbed.

'Oh, Michelle,' Mum said and cuddled me. There was nothing much she could say; the damage had been done. It was the worst Christmas I've ever had in my life. The dining room was all set up but no one ate there. The kids sat at the kitchen table but I was too distraught to have dinner.

I knew then, that our marriage was over.

Michael and I had our ups and downs but I would never ever have left him. I would never have filed for a divorce and I would have kept going, kept fighting.

Michael came home the next morning on Boxing Day and we agreed it was over. 'Well, if it's over, I'm going to announce it,' I told him.

Michael shrugged and said, 'Do what you want.'

I called one of the few people in the media I trust, who I could actually call my friend. Mark Hollinshead is managing director of the *Trinity Mirror* and the *Daily Record*. He could immediately hear in my voice that something was up. 'What's wrong? Why are you wanting to see me on Boxing Day?' he asked.

'I just need to talk to you, Mark,' I fought back the tears.

'Sure, I'll meet you for a coffee at 2.30 pm,' he agreed.

I was waiting for him at the back of a wee coffee shop called Beanscene in the centre of Glasgow. As soon as Mark sat down, I burst out crying.

'What's wrong, Michelle?' he said, looking distressed. I don't think he had any idea what I was about to tell him. On the outside, Michael and I came across as the perfect couple who had managed that rare feat of holding down a marriage while running a business together. It was the image that we had projected to the media for all those years.

'Michael walked out on us on Christmas Day. The marriage is over,' I told him. He was shocked. 'I need you to help me,' I said, wiping my tears away.

'Yes, of course. What do you need me to do?' Mark asked.

I took a deep breath. 'I need you to help me write a press release.' I felt that if I didn't write something now there was a chance it could keep going and there was no going back for me now. I'd had enough. There was a way out now and I wanted to take it. Mark helped me and I felt a huge relief that I had made the decision to send it to all the news desks. I know some people reading this will think, Why did you feel you had to tell the world? By announcing to the world we were over, there was no going back, I could finally draw a line under it and move on.

I made sure there was no mention of Sam. I wasn't doing this out of spite but for closure. The press release read: 'It is with regret that we report that Mr Michael J Mone and Mrs Michelle G Mone OBE have decided to separate. There are no other parties involved and the split is amicable. Michael and Michelle's focus will be the welfare of their children, which is their main priority. They will continue to work together in their business, MJM International. This is a private matter and they would appreciate their privacy and that of their family being respected at this difficult time.'

There were paparazzi camped outside my house for days, but I kept a low profile. Unfortunately, I had a business to run, and the show had to go on – with Michael. The marriage was over but the war between Michael and me had only just begun.

Losing all that weight had given me the confidence to see that I deserved better. It was like the final piece in a jigsaw puzzle I hadn't been able to spot until now. I wasn't going to take any more shit. I confronted Sam, head on. The first day back at work, I called her down into my office.

'I'm going to ask you something, and I want you to be honest with me,' I started.

'Uh-huh, uh-huh,' she said nervously.

'You're having an affair with my husband, aren't you?' I said. I was calm and collected but seriously pissed off.

She immediately broke down crying, 'Oh, my god, I would never do that,' she said as she turned pink. 'How could you think such a thing. I would never consider going out with my boss. You are my friend. I would never do that to you. I'm having boyfriend issues too. We've split up and he won't marry me,' she went on.

I finally broke my silence. 'Okay then, if that's what you say and if it's true then I'm sorry for asking you,' I said calmly.

Sam left and my PA came in after her. 'I told you she's not having an affair with him,' my PA said.

'She is, she one-million-per cent is,' I said. I just needed to prove it now.

Sam was going to Hong Kong with Michael and our head technical and operations guys in three weeks' time to sort through some production issues at our factories. I was going to flush them out like rats. I announced to Sam: 'I think I'll come on this trip with you.' She was taken aback at first as I didn't normally come out to Hong Kong but then she acted like my best friend.

'Oh, that would be so good,' she beamed. 'We can have time together. We don't spend enough time designing. It would be so good for you to be there. I can't wait,' she gushed.

I was upset, but I was trying to trap her, so I threw on a smile. 'Okay, so you really want me to come?' I said, double-checking.

'It would be amazing,' she beamed.

'Okay, let me look at my diary,' I told her.

I rang my PA while I was in the car to see if she could look into flights. She called me back. 'I can get you on the same flight,' my PA said.

'Book it,' I said. There was no stopping me. I phoned Sam back and announced the good news. 'I'm on the same flight,' I said over loudspeaker.

I could hear the panic in her voice. 'Oh, no, oh no you can't,' she spluttered.

I trapped her. 'Sorry?' I asked.

'You can't come. I mean, we've got meetings all planned. I meant I wanted you to come, but not on this trip.'

What? 'That's not what you said to me an hour ago,' I fired back at her. I got back to my office and I went to chat to my head of sales in her room with my PA. I could see straight into Michael's office as the whole place was made up of walls of glass.

I was telling the girls that I was going to Hong Kong and then I turned around to see Michael charging out of his office. He came running like a bull towards us.

Oh fuck. Oh Jesus.

Michael grabbed me in front of everyone. 'You fucking bitch! You're not coming to Hong Kong,' he yelled. He had his briefcase with him and he slammed it into my chest. 'If you come to Hong Kong, I quit. I need to be away from you. I don't want to be with you.'

I was trembling inside. 'Sam told me she needed me there,' I said, trying to stay calm.

'Sam doesn't need you there, I don't need you there and you better cancel your flight or I'll resign,' he threatened.

I wasn't going to be bullied. 'Resign all you like,' I said.

It exploded into a massive argument. I broke down in tears. My PA and head of sales, Margaret, tried to step in, 'Enough, Michael. Leave her alone,' they begged. Michael left and the girls came rushing to my side.

Why was he so determined not to have me there?

I phoned Carol Vorderman and asked her for *that* number. 'Who's that guy you know?' I asked her for the number of her friend's private detective. I gave the detective the dates that Michael and Sam were going to Hong Kong along with flight numbers and everything he would need to get me some proof that they were together. I needed that reassurance because Michael had been telling me that I was going nuts. I needed to show my family and my friends that I wasn't making this up. I had to know that I wasn't going mad.

I counted down the days until they left, crying myself to sleep every night. I was still in the spare room while Michael slept in the master bedroom. When he left for Hong Kong I went to London for business meetings. The detective was planted at the airport, ready to capture my husband and Sam as they came off the flight.

Carol tried to cheer me up by taking me for lunch at Scott's in Mayfair. We were sitting on the terrace outside when I got a call from the private detective. 'I need to see you,' he said with urgency.

I told him I was happy for anything to be said in front of my friend, but the detective insisted on seeing me privately. He turned up at Scott's and approached our table with a big brown envelope. My heart sank like a dead weight. 'I think you should walk with me,' he said sombrely.

'There's a park across the road,' I said, leaving Carol for a moment.

It was a cold but sunny day. We walked into the park and he told me how sorry he was as he handed me the envelope. I peeled it open to find pictures of Michael snogging Sam at the airport in front of my team and pictures of her going back to his hotel room. Deep down I knew that my marriage had been over for a long time but the pain I felt when I saw the photos was indescribable. My knees buckled and I fell to the ground crying. Carol ran over and wrapped her arms around me.

As I made my way back to Scotland with the pictures in my handbag, grief turned to anger. Michael and I had been together for 22 years and he was behaving like this only four weeks after we split up. What hurt me was the deceit, the lies, and the fact he had made me out to be mad. Even my friends had started to doubt my sanity. The fact that my team were in the pictures while he was kissing made it ten times more painful.

Mum was there to give me a hug as soon as I got home, and then I told Rebecca the news. 'Your dad is seeing Sam,' I said. She was old enough to know what was really going on.

'My dad wouldn't do that,' she snapped. Rebecca phoned Michael on his mobile and put him on loudspeaker.

'Listen, darling, I swear on your life I'd never do that to you, I'd never kiss Sam. She works for me,' he promised.

More lies.

Rebecca turned on me. 'My dad said you need to be sectioned. You need to see a doctor,' she shouted, echoing her father's words.

I had the pictures in my bag, but I couldn't let on until Michael got back because I wanted to get him first. My head was all over the place. I cried out that my own daughter didn't believe me and then I just saw red. Him lying to Rebecca, our daughter, was the final straw. I just went mad, absolutely crazy.

I charged through the kitchen, grabbing a knife and a keyring and I went to town on Michael's brand new Porsche Panamera in our driveway. Michael was so anal about his cars: if I scraped a wheel he would go on about it for a week. I swear he cared more about those cars than me. You fucker, I thought as I scratched his beloved £100k Porsche to shreds.

I charged next door to my guesthouse that I'd let Sam live in, out of the kindness of my heart. All her clothes were crumpled at the bottom of the wardrobe. I was shocked at the state of the place. Michael was OCD about cleanliness just like me. How could he find a girl who leaves her room like this attractive? I scooped the clothes up into my arms and threw every single item of hers out of the window and into the garden. I picked up the dressing table and threw that onto the drive too. I was like a banshee.

Meanwhile, Rebecca and my mum were screaming for me to stop. 'You can't do this, Mum,' Rebecca cried.

'I've done it,' I said dusting my hands off.

'You're mad. He's not having a affair,' Rebecca shouted, as she started collecting Sam's clothes into black bin bags.

I knew Michael was about to land and I'd sent a text message to him saying I'd caught him red-handed. I kept ringing Sam's phone until she picked up. Finally, I heard her voice. 'You bitch, you lied to me. You said you were not having an affair with my husband,' I screamed.

'I need to explain,' she stuttered. 'It's not like that. It only started a few days ago,' she said.

'You're a fucking liar and you're fired,' I blasted. 'Don't dare come near me, or my kids again.' I watched through the window as Michael pulled into the driveway. The first thing he was raging about was his car.

He came running in and grabbed me. 'My fucking car!' he shouted.

Rebecca was screaming as my mum separated us.

'You'll pay for that! You'll pay for that!' he yelled.

'You're lucky I didn't set fire to it, you fucker,' I told him.

'I'm calling the police.' Michael reached for the phone.

23

WAR OF
THE ROSES

Never look back.

'Michelle! Is it true you attacked your husband's car after you found out he was having an affair?' a journalist shouted from behind my electric gates. The press had found out about the car because Michael had reported me to the police. Someone close to me must have tipped them off about Sam. I had dozens of paparazzi camped outside my house shouting my name.

I put on my sunglasses to hide my bloodshot eyes and got in my black Range Rover. 'Michelle! Michelle!' they shouted as I drove off. The paps all took pictures of me in the front seat with a face like thunder.

Overnight, everything began to fall apart. Our nanny of ten years left, the housekeeper left and key people from my team just upped and left. My life came crashing down around me. Why was I getting the hard time? Michael was the one who had run off with another woman. Of course, he denied it. Michael told my operations director on the flight to Hong Kong that he had fallen in love with Sam in the 14 days following the split. But he and I had been married for 20 years. You don't fall in love in two weeks. He issued a statement to the press: 'There was no affair and what is happening now is private. Prior to our split there was no relationship. If anyone is saying that is the reason for the split, that's untrue.'

I went back to the office and things were a nightmare because the staff didn't know what was happening. Everyone was walking on eggshells and I felt really sorry for them. I couldn't believe it when I got a letter from Sam's lawyer. They said I'd sacked her without going through the correct procedures and that she was going to take me to a tribunal for unfair dismissal. What was I supposed to do? Sit down and design with her? I would have stuck the needles and scissors up her arse! I hired my own lawyer rather than go through the company because I didn't want anyone connected to Michael dealing with Sam's claim.

'You might as well just pay her off,' he advised. She wasn't the only cost. I had to pay Michael £8,000 for the damage to his car.

On the flip side, I got a lot of support from the public. The magazines wrote, 'Way to go, Michelle', for trashing his Porsche. Okay, yeah, for those ten minutes it took me to destroy it I did feel amazing, but the hangover from the fighting was killing me. I was really scared, upset and frightened because I'd never known anything other than being married to Michael. I'd never been on my own before and all my friends were married. I was desperately worried about what was to come for me, my kids and for the future of the business.

I decided I had to get away from the all the media attention and the heartache. I spoke to my friend Andrea, and her footballer husband, John Barnes, who used to play for Liverpool. They invited me to visit them in Dubai. I remember being in the airport lounge with Declan and Bethany (Rebecca wanted to stay at home with her friend), and suddenly feeling incredibly lost. I picked up the phone to my mum and dad. 'What am I doing?' I burst into tears. 'I'm so lonely. I'm never going to meet anyone. I'm always going to be on my own. I'm going to be on my own when I'm 65 with ten cats and I hate cats,' I blubbered.

I heard my mum sigh deeply at the other end. 'Michelle, just relax. Just have a good time with the kids,' she said. 'When you're not looking, it will happen.'

'Okay,' I sniffed. It was enough to calm me down and get us all on the flight.

The sunshine helped, as did being a million miles away from my troubles with just my kids. On the third day, after much persuasion, I finally found the courage to be around other people and I agreed to go out for dinner with John, Andrea, and some of their friends. I did my hair and my make-up and I helped the kids choose outfits. When we arrived, John and Andrea had a seat waiting for me next to one of their friends, Carl French.

Carl and I had a bit of common ground – Carl's wife had left him the year before and he was going through a separation. We didn't spend our time drowning our sorrows. Far from it – we got on like a house on fire. He was 6ft tall with dark hair and he was a handsome guy. He made me laugh constantly; it was the first time I'd laughed since God knows when. I felt like my spark came back that night. 'It was so lovely meeting you,' he said and kissed me on the cheek after we finished dinner. I didn't want the night to end but I was too shy to say anything. I took the kids back to our hotel and then I met up with Andrea for a girly chat. Bethany came with me while Declan did his own thing in the hotel complex.

Ring ring. Declan was calling me. 'Hi, what's up?' I answered.

'Hello, it's Carl,' came the reply. Carl had bumped into Declan at our hotel and used my son's phone to call me. 'Where are you?' he said. My heart raced. I felt like a teenager all over.

'I'm just with Andrea having a drink,' I said and blushed.

'Why don't you come back to your hotel and we can have a drink?' he suggested.

'Go go,' Andrea was mouthing to me.

So I met Carl at my hotel bar while Declan and Bethany went up to bed. A few drinks later we headed to the nightclub part of the hotel complex. We laughed, we danced and then we headed to the beach to watch the sunrise. We sat on the sand talking until 7 am and it was magical. Carl then leant over and kissed me. It felt amazing to be kissed and it felt amazing to be wanted after all those years of feeling lonely and being made to feel ugly.

Wow! Someone actually finds me attractive.

I left him on the beach and I went back to my hotel room with a skip in my step. Five hours later, I still couldn't get to sleep so I went down to the pool. Who did I see there? Carl.

From that moment on, we were inseparable. I didn't sleep with him though. You can imagine there was quite a build-up when he took me away to Rome for a weekend not long after. I remember being so nervous in the hotel bathroom while he waited for me in the bedroom. I was wearing my sexiest Ultimo underwear and I checked myself from every angle in the mirror. My heart was racing at 100 miles an hour. I took a deep breath and opened the door.

'You've got an amazing body,' Carl whispered in my ear as he kissed me.

Really? Seriously?

Somewhere there was still a fat and unloved person inside me.

Carl kept going on about my body and my smile as we lay in bed together and I was a bit shocked. I'd never had that before. It was like a dream for me to have a man think these things. I never felt like a woman with Michael, I felt masculine around him. Michael had never said anything to make me feel wanted but Carl made me feel sexy. Carl resuscitated my heart. Sadly, I just wasn't ready for a relationship. I had so many issues to deal with and so many things to sort out at home and with my business. If I were to meet him now, the scenario would be different.

I came home to face the battle of my life. I went to war with Michael over the company and over our house. Michael refused to move out. Anyone reasonable who'd had an affair would have left me to have the house with the kids. But Michael had so much nerve. He told me that *I* had to move out and that *I* should get a flat.

'How dare you make me get a flat,' I said, 'this is my home

with my kids.' I was determined that I wasn't going to leave
and I fought with him night and day. It was like *The War
of the Roses* in which Michael Douglas and Kathleen Turner
try everything to get each other to leave the house and end
up swinging from the chandelier. In fact, we had a massive
chandelier ourselves – shipped over from Miami. It was so big
that we had had to take the front door off to get it inside. We
could have done a remake of that film, I swear to God: it was
that awful.

It started as a race to the master bedroom. I was fed up of
sleeping in the spare bedroom because it was really hurting
my back. Why should he have the best bed in the house after
everything? Whoever got to the bedroom first, got the bed. I
would do things to wind him up. I put his favourite shirts and
cufflinks in the bin. I took things that really meant a lot to him
and chucked them out. I let down his car tyres. I cut holes in all
his boxer shorts.

'She'll have to look at your holey arse now,' I chuckled as
he raged at me. I wanted to disrupt his life in every way
possible because it made me feel better. I've never done anything
like that in my life before. It was my way of getting my
hurt out.

*You've hurt me so badly. I've given you three amazing kids
and 22 years of my life and I worked my arse off. I didn't even
have proper maternity leave and all you've done our whole
married life is cause me grief. I should have left you so many
times, you fucker, and now you're going to have to pay a
wee bit.*

I remember overhearing Michael tell the kids he was going
to a wedding with Sam. The next morning I waited for Michael

to leave the kitchen and then I slipped some laxatives into his coffee. 'Have a nice time,' I said, smiling sweetly as he walked past me and reached for his cup. God only knows if it worked!

Michael probably did things to me too because quite a lot of my things went missing. We lived together under the same roof for eight months after we split up. Can you believe it? We would never be in the same room for longer than a few minutes though. We couldn't be – we would have killed each other! He'd come in and I'd leave. I'd walk in and he'd storm off. Thank god Sam never stepped foot inside that house again. Who knows what would have happened? I offered to buy Michael out of the house at full market value.

'Over my dead body are you ever going to get this house!' he shouted.

'I don't understand you. You're the one who caused this. Why can't I buy my home from you? I want it as a base for me and the kids. You don't want it,' I said, trying to reason with him.

I would have redesigned it. I would have made it a new home. I wanted it because my priority was providing a stable place for the kids to live and making sure they were disrupted as little as possible.

In the end Michael and I agreed that we would alternate weeks at the house. I would spend one week in a hotel and he would spend one week at his parents' place. The day I was to leave, Michael was a total prick to me. He really upset me but instead of going to my room and crying, I got even.

I crept up to the master bedroom and I pulled back the luxurious throw. I got a bucket of water, and threw it over

Michael's side of the bed. It was soaking wet. I made the bed again and placed the pillows perfectly with the zips down. I left the house and an hour or so later I received raging text messages: 'You fucking bitch. My side of the bed is soaking wet. I'm going to phone the police and have you arrested.'

'Give it your best shot,' I said, laughing. The kids phoned to ask why I did it. 'He deserves it,' I said. I couldn't believe Michael was going to my kids after what he had done with my designer.

But looking back, I can see I was going through a very selfish time when I only cared about getting back at Michael. My priority was the children and I should have thought more about the effect it would have on them. Those things I did upset my kids and I didn't mean to upset them when it was Michael I wanted to get to. Hindsight is a wonderful thing. I have said I never regret anything in life but maybe I shouldn't have done those things. I can say now that revenge isn't worth it because it just comes back to bite you on the arse. I ended up becoming the bad one when I wasn't in the beginning.

It wasn't my only battle. I was also fighting Michael for the company that I'd created in 1996. Who was going to buy who out? We went to war in the day and again in the evening, just as we had been doing privately for years. But now our fight had become public and the company value crashed through the floor. It was like someone had thrown a grenade into our business. The buyers didn't know what was going on so they didn't order stock. No decisions were made within the office. It was awful for the brand.

Then all of a sudden, Michael dealt a low blow. 'You're fired,'

I'm so proud of my children and who they are today. It hasn't been an easy ride but Rebecca (*top left*), Bethany (*top right*) and Declan (*bottom*) have given me the determination to be a success.

My inventions have
been modelled by a
number of amazing
models over the years.
Along with Penny
Lancaster and Rachel
Hunter, Sarah Harding
(*above*) and Mel B
(*right*) have both been
the 'faces' of Ultimo…

[© Getty Images]

...as well as Luisana Lopilato and the late Peaches Geldof.

I received an OBE in 2011. It was another proud moment in my career.

[© Getty Images]

I underwent a life-changing moment in 2005 and decided I didn't want to hide behind my business any longer. A few years later I modelled for Ultimo and I have never looked back.

[© Dan Kennedy]

I'm extremely proud of my modelling career: here I am on a photoshoot for *Hello* magazine. *[© Dan Kennedy]*

I've met some amazing people (and a few heroes!) during my career as a motivational speaker, including Al Pacino (*above*) and Sylvester Stallone (*below*).

My life has been full of ups and downs and I'm so looking forward to the future. I bought U-Tan from Ultimo and got back on the motivational speaker circuit. I'm excited about inspiring other people to fight to the top!

he said, pointing his finger at me as if he was Lord Alan Sugar. 'I've got one share more than you,' he smirked. Michael had 48 per cent and I had 47 per cent.

How the hell did that happen?

Michael dealt with all the legal side of things, so it must have been when we bought Tom Hunter and Ian Grabiner out. There had been an extra share floating about. 'Fuck you,' I spat. The gloves were off.

Michael may have had one more share than me, but he didn't have enough to control the business. He needed more than 50 per cent to be making decisions like that. I needed to find an ally – I needed to get Tom Walker on my side. Tom was a silent shareholder who owned 5 per cent. He'd come on board at the same time as Tom Hunter and Ian, but he hadn't wanted to be bought out in 2004.

Tom could go with me or he could go with Michael.

I managed to convince him to back me and together we had more power than Michael.

Take that, you fucker.

Round two involved Michael trying to buy me out. 'Go for it, you'll never raise the money,' I said. I then tried to buy Michael out, but he wanted a ridiculous sum.

For the first time in my life, I began to drink. I downed a bottle of white wine a night to numb the pain. I would cry myself to sleep and some nights, when I couldn't bear to be alone, I would crawl into Rebecca's bed. I was in a very dark, lonely place, but I had to fight for survival and I had to fight for my kids and my family – and for the company too.

I brought all the team together and I said, 'Listen, guys, I'm going to save your jobs,' I promised. They were so worried; they had bills to pay and families to support. 'I promise you with all my heart.' I fought back the tears.

Whatever punch Michael threw, I still got up the next day ready for battle. I'd fight all day long. You're not going to kill me, I thought. Michael may have been a university graduate and he may have been more intelligent than me, but I had more fight than him and more stamina. It was like the biggest boxing match in history.

Round three – the company went up for sale. Offers came flooding in from people who wanted to work with me alone and not Michael. One of the four main contenders wanted me to move to Hong Kong so that was a 'No' because I would never leave my kids.

'I want you to sign this. It's our only way out,' Michael shouted about the offer. He was going mental over it. Michael was desperate for the company to be sold because we had director guarantees with the bank. What that meant was, if I didn't buy Michael out, he was going to have to write the bank a big cheque for a million quid.

'I'm not signing,' I said and crossed my arms. There was no way I was agreeing to it because all these buyers wanted to lock me in with them and I didn't like them enough to give Michael a free ticket out of jail. 'I'm not doing it your way,' I said and stamped my foot. 'You want me to sign up with anyone that will give you the money but you don't give a shit that I have to work with them for several years while you get away.'

The company continued to fall to pieces and the banks were getting concerned. We didn't have long until we went under. When I closed my eyes I could see it crashing all the way to the bottom. It was just the way it had been all those years ago with the stock problems.

History was repeating itself.

24

BRA
WARS

*Life is like a marathon. You just have
to keep going until you reach that line.*

'I'm going to Sri Lanka,' I announced to my mum when
I phoned her from the plane. I was minutes from take off.
A request had come through in October 2012 for me to give
one of my motivational speeches. I jumped at the chance to get
away from the chaos, if only for a few days.

'No, you're not. You're about to lose your company. You're
about to lose your life. You can't do this speech,' she screeched.

'Mum, I need to go. I love you and I'll see you when I'm
back.' I hung up. Something inside me was saying I needed to
go. I trusted my instinct. It turned out to be a hell of a journey
as I was delayed in my stop over in Dubai and then I got stuck
in a three-hour traffic jam to my hotel. I'd been travelling
for 24 hours and was desperate for a shower and a change of
clothes when the hosts broke the news that I had to be on stage
in ten minutes.

I rushed to the toilet to throw up. I looked awful. But there was no time to do my hair and my make-up; I just had to get out there and get on with it. I was running on empty as I made my way up on stage. The room fell silent as hundreds of eyes locked onto me, waiting for me to speak. I took a deep breath and stepped into the spotlight. I gave them the speech of my life.

'In the next few months, I don't know where I'll be. I don't know if the company will still be there,' I said as I fought back the tears. 'But what I do know is that I'm so passionate about the brand.' I spoke from the heart. I told them my story and there were people in the audience crying as I described how hard I'd had to fight.

As I left the stage, the organisers of the event led me down the hall to meet someone who had the potential to help me.

He reached his hand out and said 'I'm Mahesh Amalean, I chair the board of MAS Holdings, we manufacture intimate apparel for some of the biggest brands around the world.' Mahesh was in his late 50s and such a gentleman.

I knew immediately that I wanted to work with him. He was the missing piece in the jigsaw.

I flew back to Glasgow with a fire in my belly. I'd reached a point where I knew I had to take control of myself and fight for what was mine. No one was going to take away what I'd worked so hard to achieve, what I'd sacrificed so much for.

MAS started due diligence, the audit that any company has to undergo before investment. We had just a week left to go before due diligence was complete when Michael found out about MAS. The boxing gloves were back on as Michael dug his heels in and started making demands for more money and different conditions. I needed the help of the bank. I called an emergency meeting at HSBC in February 2013.

I'll never forget that day as long as I live. Ultimo was literally weeks away from going under and my future, as well as that of the brand, hinged on whether I could get Michael to leave. I woke up and threw on my armour for one last fight. I wore a sharply tailored suit that spoke volumes – it said, 'Don't mess with me'. I walked into that boardroom like I was walking onto a battlefield.

'We are weeks from going under and, Michael, you don't have another offer on the table,' I said.

I had lit his fuse. 'I don't care,' he said and started to list what he wanted.

'Well, you're not in a position to want things,' I interrupted. I reasoned with HSBC. 'Look, if Michael doesn't leave, MAS won't buy in and if they don't buy in, this company will go under and you'll lose money,' I told the directors.

The bank had to decide who to support. You could have cut the atmosphere with a knife. There was so much tension. I took a sip of water and glanced across to Michael. He was looking daggers at me.

'Okay, we've decided,' one of the directors said at last, shuffling his papers in order. They turned to Michael, 'You've got no other offers on the table so we back Michelle to go through with this offer from MAS.'

Yes. Victory.

In a nutshell, Michael was told by the bank to behave and to be fair otherwise he would have to write them a cheque for £1m. We agreed that I would buy Michael's shares and sell them on to MAS.

But Michael just couldn't admit defeat. 'Okay, I'll sell you my shares but I want you to sign a non-embarrassment clause.' This meant that if I sold his shares within a certain amount of time – he specified three years – I had to give him half the profit.

I'd had enough. My blood boiled. 'I'm not signing anything like that,' I said, pointing at his face. It was frightening to watch his reaction.

I bought Michael out at 10 o'clock in the morning. I'll never disclose what I bought Michael out for. All I will say is that the papers reported it was £24m and that isn't true. I don't know where they got that figure from.

We also agreed the paperwork for our divorce that same morning. I just wanted it all out of the way so I wouldn't have to deal with him again. We decided to put our house up for sale. That was almost the final time I saw Michael.

It was only half the battle won though. I still had to close the deal with MAS Holdings that afternoon. MAS had a list of requests to fulfill before they would buy Michael's shares and that included the resignation of board member Scott Kilday, my operations director of 12 years. I'd explained to Scott on the run up to the meeting that it wasn't personal: 'Scott, MAS have asked you to resign as a board director because they don't want anyone on the board who they don't know. If you get to know them you've got a great future ahead of you but right now there won't be a job at all unless you resign.'

Scott had agreed and, what was more, he'd gone out of his way to thank me for saving his job as his wife was about to have a third baby. I'd considered the matter done and dusted – that was, until we were minutes from wrapping up.

We were back in the boardroom. The lawyers and the accountants were going through each point. The representatives of MAS were in the room, waiting to close the deal. There had been ten items on a piece of paper that I had to agree. We were at the last point. We were waiting for Scott to send through a letter of resignation from the board. Just as we felt were about to cross the finishing line the bank got a phone call.

'Michelle, there's a Scott Kilday saying he urgently needs to speak to you.'

Oh dear god. I looked at the representatives from MAS. *I'm five minutes away from my life changing, saving everyone's job, getting my baby back and being able to move on.*

The bank representative handed me the phone. 'Hi, Scott, is it urgent?' I said.

'Er, yeah, I want to talk to you,' he said. I could tell from the tone of his voice that he was about to fuck me.

'Excuse me, everyone,' I said as I left the room. I took a deep breath and listened to what Scott had to say.

'I'm not resigning from the board,' he said, defiantly.

My heart sank. 'Scott, do you actually know what you're doing?' I wanted to shake him. It was too much to bear. 'Scott, I've fought for a year to save the business, I'm five minutes away from the line, we've ticked all nine boxes and you're the last box to tick,' I pleaded.

'Yeah, well, I'm not doing it,' he went on.

'These people won't buy in unless you step down because they don't know you and you can work to get back on the board. Why are you doing this?' I wanted to cry.

'It's a "No",' he said.

I hung up on him and walked back into the boardroom with

a heavy heart. It was over. My face must have been chalk white as I faced the room full of people.

'What's happened?' asked Eliaz, who sits on the board of directors for MAS.

'Scott won't resign as a board member.' I shook my head in despair. 'Guys, I'm sorry for wasting your time for the last four months. I gave it the fight of my life. I wanted this to go through. I really believe in this brand but, I'm sorry, it's not going to work.' All that stress and emotion that I had built up throughout the day overwhelmed me. My knees buckled and I fell to the floor in tears.

Eliaz rose to his feet. 'Michelle, come here,' he said and held out his hand.

'Uh-huh.' I looked up at him.

'Do me a favour. Phone Scott and tell him he doesn't have to resign as a board member. We've taken that point away,' he said.

'Really?' I spluttered.

'Congratulations. Welcome to MAS.' He grinned. I took his hand and rose to my feet. The battle of my life was finally over. I'd bought Michael out at 10 am on 6 February 2013 as well as negotiating our divorce and then I'd sold on his shares to MAS at 5.05 pm that same day.

I went from crying on the floor, thinking I'd lost everything, to celebrating with Cristal champagne with all the team from MAS. We went to my favourite restaurant in the world – Andrew Fairlie's Michelin starred restaurant in the Gleneagles hotel.

Bloody hell. How did I do that?

I couldn't believe it. I was so delirious that I actually passed out in the car on the way home. I felt like I had run a marathon.

I had kept running and I wouldn't stop until I got over the finish line and then I collapsed. It was the same thing that had happened when I put on the fashion show with Rod Stewart and Penny Lancaster.

My driver woke me up and carried me into my house. My legs were like jelly. I collapsed into bed and didn't wake until Mum came into my room the next morning. She'd been babysitting the kids the night before.

'What time is it?' I rubbed the sleep out of my eyes.

'It's 9am,' said Mum, glancing at her watch.

'Oh, my god.' I sat bold upright. 'I've got new partners, and I'm late.'

'Relax,' Mum laughed.

I burst out laughing. I've never relaxed in my life. I don't know how!

25

CLEAN SLATE

Always look forward.

'No peeking,' I said to the kids as I unlocked the door of our new townhouse. I'd spent months transforming a derelict four-storey Victorian building in the centre of Glasgow into our dream home. It was finally ready in August 2013, which was around the time my divorce came through – a double celebration!

I didn't want to show the kids until it was completely finished. They walked in and I covered their eyes. Bethany grinned from ear to ear when she was able to see the place. 'Mum, this is so special,' she said and hugged me. This was going to be our home, a fresh start for us all.

'Okay I'm going to give you a bit of a history lesson,' I said, leading them up the winding staircase. 'It was built in 1871 and Albert Einstein even lived here…'

'Oh, wow, the TV comes out of the end of the bed,' Declan

interrupted. He was more interested in the gadgets. I'd asked the kids how they wanted their rooms and we'd designed them together. Declan insisted he had a black and red colour scheme and Bethany wanted something very girly. Rebecca was now living away from home but there was a spare bed for whenever she wanted to stay.

I wanted my bedroom to be really relaxing and romantic and to look like my favourite hotel. I asked the Dorchester to show me around its suites and I picked one which I basically copied. This was far less flashy than my old house. The quality was there in terms of the fabrics and the furniture but I got rid of all the things I didn't need.

I could have bought a house in the same area as the last one and probably one that was the same size but I wanted a complete change. I also wanted to be around people rather than in the countryside. The kids could now walk for two minutes and be in the city centre without having to wait for me to give them a lift. Above all, the new place gave me closure. As soon as I moved in, the feeling of bitterness which used to eat me up at night vanished.

It was a new beginning for my children and me. It's hard on any kids when parents split up but my kids had to live with reading about it in the press as well and they had to cope with their dad running off with their mum's designer. The whole thing was awful and I was determined to do everything in my power to make it up to them. I started spending a lot more time with them and I kept telling them how much I loved them. I had a lot of heart-to-hearts with Rebecca because I felt she was the one who had been most affected by all that had happened.

I remember one night when she stayed over. We were sitting on her bed and I felt this overwhelming need to explain something. I love you with all my heart.' I took Rebecca's hand in mine. 'I want to work on our relationship.'

Rebecca had tears in her eyes. 'I just remember you not having as much time for me when I was growing up as you did for Bethany and Declan,' she said and started crying.

'That's just nonsense,' I said and shook my head. 'I'm never going to leave your side. I want to prove to you that throughout your life I've loved you just as much as Declan, just as much as Bethany.' I started to cry. We hugged and said how much we loved each other. It's taken a bit of time, but the two of us are now inseparable. I'd say we are like best friends.

Now that I had my kids around me and I'd won my company back, nothing could hurt me. Even the news that Michael had launched a rival company, Pendulum Apparel, with Sam as his senior designer, didn't bother me. The press went mad for it, calling it 'Bra Wars' and they constantly badgered me for my reaction. If Michael had launched the company the year before I probably would have started World War III. The truth is that as soon as I won back Ultimo I stopped caring. I didn't care about him or her any more. All I cared about were my kids and building my business up.

I was feeling so much better and happier in myself that I decided it was time to test the waters and go on some dates. I'd had a lot of friends wanting to set me up, but I'd said 'No' until now. In December 2013 my friend Michael Vaughan, who used to captain the England cricket team, texted me to find out if I was still single.

'Yeah,' I replied.

'How is someone as beautiful as you still single?' he asked.

'I've not met anyone who ticks my boxes,' I replied. I seized the opportunity.

'Have you not got any good looking pals?' I enquired.

'Yeah, I've got loads,' he replied. Michael mentioned Shane Warne.

'Oh that's the guy who used to go out with Elizabeth Hurley,' I said.

'That's right. He's such a laugh.' Michael texted back.

I couldn't remember what he looked like, so I googled Shane. 'He's quite hot,' I replied.

'I'm with him later. I'll put a word in,' he said, adding a wink to his message.

Oh, God. I felt myself blush behind the phone screen.

I got a message later that night. Shane wanted my phone number. 'Oh, my god, really?' I was shocked. Like I said before, I'm confident in my work but not when it comes to men. I was rediscovering my teenage years. 'Okay, why not?' I decided. Sometimes you've got to live a little. I gave Shane my number and that was it. For the next two months we were texting and chatting over the phone constantly. Shane was so much fun and so witty. I have to admit that I felt the odd text message did go a bit far and was too explicit to come from someone I'd never met before. I would just change t he subject.

When Shane announced he was flying into London in February, he added that he wanted to whisk me away for the weekend. I was really keen to see him but that was a 'No no' for me. 'Erm, I'm not going to go away for the weekend when I've not met you before,' I said and backed off. We arranged to meet up for a drink when he landed instead. The two months we had spent messaging and calling one another made for quite a build-up to our meeting.

I got a text message from Shane on Valentine's Day saying, 'This is my UK phone number'.

He'd arrived a day early?

'Yeah, I had to come and sort some things out with the ex,' he explained.

My brain started to go wild. *It's Valentine's Day and he's come early. Has he come early to spend the day with Liz Hurley?* 'Okay, enjoy.' I put up my guard.

I'd had messages from Shane every hour of every day for the previous two months and then the messages stopped from the morning of the 14th. I didn't hear from him at all. *God, is he getting back with her? What is he doing?* My mind was racing in a way I didn't like. He was coming to see me the next day, a Saturday. I got a message from him that morning. 'Sorry, babe, that I didn't get back to you yesterday. I was in massive discussions with the ex. Can't wait to see you tonight. It's amazing that we are finally going to see each other.'

I was staying in the Dorchester but I didn't want to meet him there because the Bafta Awards were on and there would be paparazzi lurking. 'Why don't we meet somewhere else?' I suggested.

'I won't meet you in the bar. I'll come to your room,' he said.

I had a suite with a lounge so I thought that would be okay – we could just sit and chat. I got all dressed up and did my hair and make-up. My stomach was going mad with butterflies as the time got closer to 7.30 pm. Shane was the first guy I'd been interested in since I met Carl a year earlier.

7.45 pm – Shane sent me a message saying he wasn't going to make it.

You fucker, I thought. 'That's really disappointing. It's a Saturday night and I'm all dressed up and you're sending me a text message 15 minutes after you are supposed to be here. Think that's a bit rude,' I snapped.

How could you do this? I would have never been so rude to someone.

'I'll promise I'll make it up to you tomorrow, if you'll let me see you,' he begged.

'Yeah, whatever.' I blanked him. No guy treats a woman like that. I went out with my friends instead.

I was relaxing in my hotel the next day, when I got a message from Shane. 'I'm on my way to see you,' he announced.

I'd had enough. 'I don't know if you should,' I told him, having seen pictures of him in all the papers getting out of Liz Hurley's car. 'Look, are you back with her?' I said. There was no way I was going near a taken man. I'd experienced, first hand, how painful that is.

'I promise you, I'm not and I haven't been with her,' he said. 'We've been in discussions for hours since I got back. Please believe me.'

He touched a nerve. *Come on, Michelle, maybe you should stop being so hard. Maybe you should let down your guard and give him the benefit of the doubt?* Finally, after all that build-up, he walked into my hotel suite on Sunday.

We opened a bottle of champagne and chatted. It wasn't the sort of conversation I'd been expecting. He chain-smoked about 35 cigarettes and I hate smoke. I thought he was a great fun guy, but I knew then and there that he wasn't for me.

After about an hour, Shane got restless. 'Can we go next door to the bedroom?' he said, suggestively.

'Er, no. I'm not that kind of girl,' I said. 'And I've got a Radio 5 Live interview to do.' Shane got papped coming out of the Dorchester after someone tipped off the press that he had been up to my room.

Boom, I was back in the news – 'Shane Warne in hotel romp with Michelle Mone'. I had TV crews camped outside my door when I got back to Glasgow. I was offered a lot of money to speak about what had happened but I didn't say a word because I thought I'd rise above it and move on. And that's exactly what I've done, moved on. I've learnt a valuable lesson. I'll never start texting a guy without meeting him first. Shane wasted two months of my time, quite frankly. I thought he was a good guy, a great father, a funny guy and I liked the fact he was Australian. But he wasn't my type in the end. He's a bit too wild for me.

The reason why I'm speaking about this in my book is because I felt I couldn't leave out things that had been all over the press. My book is about telling the truth.

I think I'll let things happen naturally from now on. I do want love and I feel I'm finally ready to find it. My ideal partner would be someone who isn't intimidated by who I am, who is equal to me and likes a laugh, just the way that I do. Not much to ask, is it? I think that what all women really want is simply to be loved. I've never been with a man who has treated me like a lady and loved me. That's what I'd really like but it has to be with the right man and if he isn't the right one then I'm fine by myself. I know it will happen one day and I know that special guy will make my life complete but I'm not willing to settle for second best.

26

LIKE MOTHER LIKE DAUGHTER

If you fail to plan, then plan to fail.

'We can't find a model with 32E breasts.' The girls in the marketing department needed someone to show off Ultimo's new Fuller Bust bra range. Good models with big boobs are hard to come by. 'What are we going to do?' They were tearing their hair out. The range featured cups ranging from a DD to a G and we had just days to put on a show for buyers. As luck would have it, my daughter Rebecca walked into the office looking for me. One of the marketing girls piped up, 'Rebecca, what bra size are you?' she inquired.

Rebecca looked puzzled. 'Er, 32E,' she said as she blushed.

'Oh, my god,' the girls squealed with joy. Before I knew it, they were asking if Rebecca could model the new Fuller Bust for the buyers. I hadn't said a word at this point. Rebecca looked to me for reassurance.

'It's just for the buyers. It's fine if you want to do it,' I said.

Rebecca said she would and went on to model for us at the Dorchester. She was a little star in the making. She looked beautiful, in a really natural way, with her long blonde hair and perfect figure. The buyers came up to me and told me how amazing my daughter looked. 'The bras fit her perfectly,' they gushed.

I was a very proud mum. However, that was the end of the modelling as far as I was concerned. I've always tried to shield my kids from the press. 'Home time,' I said to Rebecca, as the show came to an end. 'We can pick up some food on the way.' I was back in my mother role.

But the girls in the office couldn't stop talking about it the next day. We had to find a 32E model to be the face of the new range. 'Rebecca, Rebecca,' they chorused.

I sighed deeply. 'Look, she's never modelled before,' I reasoned.

'But neither had you and look how your pictures turned out,' they went on. Rebecca was the spitting image of me as I had been at her age. They wouldn't let it drop. They asked Rebecca and eventually convinced her that she was the best model for the job. I didn't want any involvement. I was worried that people would think I was using my daughter for PR and exposing her for my own interests. More importantly, I was worried that Rebecca's life would change overnight and that she wouldn't be ready for it. Rebecca is very quiet and sensitive and highly intelligent. Publicity isn't her thing; she's shunned the celebrity world all her life. She also backed away from previous opportunities to take the limelight through singing.

Rebecca has an amazing voice. Not long before the modelling came up I took her down to meet my friend Yvie Burnett who trains the singers for TV shows like *The Voice* and *The*

X-Factor. Evie said that Rebecca was incredible and that she had a serious shot at getting a record deal. But Rebecca backed away from the idea of moving to London. So the modelling had to be her decision.

'Are you sure you want to do this?' I asked. Rebecca had a serious lack of confidence and it was something I worked on all the time. I'd suffered so much with a lack of self-confidence and she was the last person I wanted to see suffer in the same way.

'Yes, Mum. I really want to do it,' she said.

As the day of the shoot grew nearer, I became more anxious. I was more nervous about this than any other shoot. Rebecca was so dedicated to doing a good job. She was in the gym working out every single day. Her body was to die for. I chose Dan, the photographer I'd always used and the man who photographed me. Of course, there were a lot of 'like mother like daughter' comments going around.

We rented a plush house in London where there was a team of 20 waiting to transform my girl into a model. And then I got the phone call. Rebecca had missed her flight from Glasgow. Or rather, she had pulled out because Michael was annoyed at her for modeling for Ultimo. 'You do this photo shoot if you want to do it. Don't do it if you are feeling pressured,' I said. I didn't want to be piggy in the middle between Rebecca and her dad.

'I want to do this, I do,' she insisted.

We got her on the next flight to London but she missed that too. The pressure started to mount.

'I told you, I didn't want anything to do with this,' I snapped. I could understand why Rebecca was stressed and I would have completely understood if she wanted to pull out, but the to-ing and fro-ing was doing my head in. Rebecca kept insisting she wanted to do it and, three flights later, she finally arrived in London with a smile on her face. I swear to god I could have killed her if I didn't love her so much.

We were now running out of time and the pressure was even greater. Rebecca was nervous and she took way longer than she should with her hair and make-up. 'Hurry up. Time is money and we have so much to do today,' I said as my business brain took over. I think my team was too nervous to push Rebecca because she was my daughter. 'If this was any other shoot, you'd be telling the model to move her arse. She needs to get moving.' I told them. I'd never been in this position before, mixing business with personal stuff. I felt way out of my comfort zone.

Am I Michelle, the tough bra tycoon, or Michelle the mum?

'Leave me alone, Mum,' Rebecca told me. I think I was winding her up.

Rebecca finally came into the room in her dressing gown. To be honest, I thought we'd made a mistake. Rebecca was like a lump of wood. She spread her fingers apart like a fan. Her poses were something like you'd see in the 1970s.

Jesus Christ, she's really bad. I love my daughter to pieces, but we had at least £50,000 tied up in this shoot. I turned to one of my marketing girls and whispered in her ear, 'Get on the phone right now to a modelling agency and get me a 32E model. Whatever it takes, I need her here, right away, on standby,' I said. I was panicking, which in turn was making Rebecca panic even more. It was snowballing.

Dan turned to me and gave me what for. 'Get out, Michelle.' he pointed to the door. He'd been through the whole drama with me in 2010 and knew how to handle a Mone.

'Dan, we have got to save this shoot,' I said. I was flustered.

'We've got deadlines, we've got this launch around the corner and we've got the magazines expecting the pictures. Give me a moment.'

I took Rebecca aside in the next room. 'Rebecca, you know I love you so much, which is why I'm going to give you a few tips,' I said. 'Right, relax your hands... Do this,' I said, shaking my hands. Rebecca copied me. 'That's it! We don't want your fingers spread out like bloody octopus legs.'

'Okay, Mum,' Rebecca said, practising her moves in the mirror.

Dan crept up behind me. 'That's it, Michelle, out,' he said firmly and ushered me to the door.

'What do you mean?' I protested.

'Get out and leave it to me.' Dan wasn't taking 'No' for an answer.

An hour passed and I started pacing up and down the hallway. After another hour I wanted to pull my hair out with anxiety. I was just reaching for the door handle when Dan appeared. He had a big grin on his face. 'Come here a minute,' he said and showed me the preview images on his camera's screen.

Oh, my god. The pictures were breathtaking. And I'm not just saying that because I'm Rebecca's mum. The images looked as if they'd been photoshopped – that's how flawless she seemed. Tears started to collect in my eyes. I was so incredibly proud of her. How could she have gone from posing so badly to looking like this? I thought she must have had a glass of wine. 'Well done,' I said, grabbing her for a hug.

'Thanks, Mum,' she said and looked very relieved.

I chose about 40 of the best photos of Rebecca – I always make the picture selection because I know that just one bad photo can have a serious impact on the brand. I won't allow legs open shots at Ultimo. We are not that kind of brand – quite frankly, it's vulgar. We are sexy and sophisticated. I was more vigilant than I had ever been when it came to Rebecca. I didn't want any of them looking sexual. I wasn't having the public look at my daughter in that way.

I always knew the shots of Rebecca were going to provoke a massive response from the press. The marketing team weren't sure. 'Well, we don't really know if it will go that big,' they said.

'Are you crazy? She's the daughter I haven't let model up until now. It will explode,' I laughed. And the shoot did explode. Her pictures went right across the world. Rebecca's phone was ringing off the hook as everyone approached her, from *Hello* magazine to the producers of *I'm a Celebrity... Get Me Out of Here*. Rebecca couldn't believe it and it gave her an incredible confidence boost.

I was dealing with all Rebecca's press when my life took a completely different turn. Seven months earlier I'd been invited alongside other Scottish people to 10 Downing Street to give my honest views about independence. Scotland's referendum on whether or not to stay with the UK was due in the autumn of 2014 and it was no secret that I was a 'No'. I thought it would be really bad for businesses and I believed that Scotland could not survive on its own. I love Scotland so much and fly the flag everywhere I go when travelling around the world, but this wasn't a passionate vote. I had even said that I would move to England if it happened. Everyone in the room that day was telling the prime minister that he was doing an amazing job with the Better Together campaign. I was listening to them all thinking, You arse lickers. How can you be so fake? Tell him how it really is.

I tried to bite my tongue as David Cameron made his way around the room. He finally approached me and said, 'Michelle, what's your opinion?'

I looked at him, and then I looked at everyone else there.

Do I go along with all these people and play it safe? Or do I just go for it?

All my life, I've gone for it. 'Do you know what the problem is, David?' I blurted.

Did she really say that? Everyone looked horrified because I hadn't addressed him as 'Prime Minister'. I'm not kidding, I heard cutlery fall to the plates. I suddenly felt bad but it was too late to turn back. 'Your problem is that you're not communicating with wee Mary from Govan.' I went on. 'She doesn't understand what you are saying. She thinks you are this posh bloke in London. Wee Mary from Govan is looking for the answers and you need to come down to her level and explain to her what to do.' The prime minister was gobsmacked. He was just staring at me as I rattled on. 'And your Better Together campaign is rubbish and isn't working. Whoever is running that campaign needs to understand what's going on in the real world.'

Cameron didn't let on if I had offended him. He politely smiled and nodded.

I was sure I had annoyed him so it was my turn to be speechless when Ramsay Jones, the prime minister's special advisor for Scotland, contacted me to ask if I'd be interested in helping the Better Together campaign. There was just over a month to go before the vote on 18 September. David Cameron wanted me to be the focus for TV and press interviews.

Me, involved in politics? Michelle Mone, who left school with no qualifications? I couldn't believe it. At first I thought I wouldn't risk my reputation. I didn't just want to be a rent-a-gob. But as the campaign moved on I realised that the 'No' campaign were losing ground. The Scottish National Party's independence drive was way ahead. I thought, It's shocking that the people of Scotland are turning this into a question of passion rather than realism. I'm a realist, so I decided to step up. As soon as I said 'Yes', I was fully committed. I'm all or nothing.

I got to know the Better Together campaign members. I whipped them into shape a wee bit. Then numerous interviews started coming through for me – a total of 54 requests. The Better Together organisers tried to tell me which ones to do. I wasn't having any of it. I questioned their reasoning on each point. 'No, why would I do that?' and 'What impact will that have?' In the end, I confidently selected my own interviews. I was on fire. I discovered a side to myself I never knew before. For the first time in my life I put Ultimo on the back burner. I was in full campaign mode.

Next, I had MPs coming to my house to prep me for the interviews. We had three weeks left before the referendum and I had days to get to grips with the SNP's blueprint for independence, in the shape of a 649-page white paper. I was at politics boot camp – training all day, every day. They literally sat me down in a chair and read me the white paper. They made me memorise the parts I needed to raise in debates.

I was put through my paces by a team consisting of the shadow foreign secretary for Labour, Douglas Alexander, former defence secretary John Reid and the prime minister's special advisor for Scotland, Ramsay Jones. 'Michelle, we are going to interview you,' Douglas said. 'How much did SNP say in the white paper that oil is trading at per barrel?'

Think, Michelle, think.

'$113,' I fired back. I felt like I was in the hot seat on a quiz show.

'And how much is it worth now?

'$96,' I blurted.

'Okay, pass.' Douglas smiled.

Because I'm dyslexic I'm all about pictures rather than words, so I stuck drawings up all over my kitchen of the key points I needed to remember. I would open the cupboard to get a mug and there would be a statistic on the door. My work is all about making products look amazing through colour and design and I took that approach to my training. I also kept asking questions. By the end of the four-week boot camp, I'm not kidding, I was a full-blown politician. The MPs laughed that I had a new career after Ultimo. I barely had time to catch my breath before I was sent out into the battlefield.

'Sky News is looking for someone to speak about why we need to keep our union together. We've nominated you,' announced Douglas Alexander.

'Me?' I stuttered. I was going to be representing the MPs on live TV. Fear struck in my heart as it suddenly became real. Sky News Live had set up a base outside the Scottish parliament. As I was on my way I was told the producers were to feature another businesswoman representing the SNP viewpoint. I was also told she was well-educated. She had gone to university and knew loads about politics. I was caught off-guard – this was not what I thought I was going to be doing for my first live interview. I panicked as I suddenly felt out of my depth. I can put a bra together better than anyone but when you ask me about the economy... I was so out of my comfort zone. I told myself to pretend I was wee Mary from Govan who needed answers.

I walked up the stairs of Sky News's temporary live studio overlooking parliament. 'Are you ready for the live debate?' the producer said as she put the microphone on me.

'No, I'm not. What are you trying to do?' I snapped. I wasn't going to be doing a debate.

'It's okay. The presenter, Adam Boulton, will interview you and then go to the other lady and then you two will have a bit of a debate,' she said.

'No, you will not. You will interview *her* and then you will interview me,' I said. I stood my ground and I won. When Sky News explained to the other interviewee that there would be no debate, she went mental. She was a tiny wee woman with a very loud voice.

'I want a debate with *her*.' She was pointing and screaming. For pity's sake, I thought, as I heard her mouthing off. The next thing I knew, she came charging up to me like a rhino. 'I want them to go to you first and then interview me.'

'I'm not going to speak to you at all,' I said calmly. 'I don't even know who you are. I'm really sorry, who are you?' So she told me who she was. 'Good luck to you and your business,' I said politely, 'but I've never heard of you and I'm not having a debate with you.'

I had to be quick on my feet dealing with all these highly educated people. I found it really scary. I hadn't gone to university and I don't read about politics much. I was dying inside but I wasn't about to give up the fight.

She then started arguing with Adam Boulton, the presenter.

'Oh, please, shut up. I'm coming to you first,' he said.

'I want you to go to Michelle first,' she screamed. It was a circus. Everyone was screaming seconds from going live. 'I want you to go to *her* first…'

'Welcome to Edinburgh,' Adam said, trying to drown her out. She went first and then Adam asked me to comment on her points.

The whole time she was mouthing off in the background: 'I don't want her commenting on my answers.'

This was probably the most composed I'd had to be so far in the campaign. I had to be calm, collected and remember my points. I was friendly and relaxed with Adam. 'Look, the polls open in the morning and we don't even know what currency we are going to have yet. There's too much deficit – it's a massive £6 billion…' I was stating pure business facts – just because I said 'No' didn't mean I wasn't passionate about Scotland. We were all passionate about Scotland but I knew if we became independent it would be much harder for business.

As I spoke to Adam Boulton, a demonstration was breaking out below me. SNP supporters were banging on the fences round the scaffolding that held up the temporary studio. I could hear the banging as I was trying to speak. So I said my piece and was happy with it but my opponent was still raging. 'Good luck with your business,' I said and tried to shake her hand.

'Don't touch me,' she snarled. She needed to calm down. It wasn't personal, it was business, and she should have known that, being a businesswoman too.

I started walking down the stairs and security came running after me. 'Michelle, you can't go out there,' they said.

'Why?'

'There's a demonstration out there, and they are waiting for you.' The crowd had been watching the coverage on their mobile phones and were shouting that they wanted to get me.

Jesus. Deep breath. The security team marched me around the whole park to where they had a car for me. It was a scary, scary moment. I'm not talking about a couple of people waiting. There were hundreds out there, banging away at the fences.

'Get your head down,' they said as I drove off. I was headed straight to another TV show. It was battle after battle after battle. I put myself right out there – no other businessperson was doing that. I was scared it would affect my career and people warned it could ruin me, but I couldn't give up in what I believed in. I kept fighting the whole way.

My mum and dad helped keep me going. I thought they would tell me to stop, but instead they said, 'You need to tell the people of Scotland what this is all about. You are an East End girl and you need to say independence is too much of a risk for our nation.'

I got death threats on Twitter and letters to my house: 'You better stop now or you're getting it.' I was called a bitch, a cow and a slut but I still fought on. It took a lot out of me and I was already paranoid about safety after the carjacking. I hired a security guard to protect the house. I wouldn't walk anywhere on my own, I wouldn't even walk around the busy shopping area of Buchanan Street. I double-checked all the alarms and cameras before bed and I got a lock fitted on my bedroom. I had the kids chauffeured to and from school. I had an escape route from the house worked out for all of us. As with business, I believe you should always have a plan in case it goes wrong. I blocked over 350 users on Twitter who were writing abuse.

At times I did think, Should I give up? I've got three amazing kids – am I putting them at risk? But I couldn't give up – it isn't in my nature.

Keep going, must keep going.

I wasn't going to be bullied any more. I wanted to say to people, 'This is my opinion and you may not think I'm right, but I'm entitled to have it. As everyone is.'

I did 27 live TV interviews in the final 48 hours before the polls closed. I didn't sleep and I barely stopped for food or drink – I was running on pure adrenaline. I can't tell you how nerve-wracking it was in those final hours because the outcome was touch and go. Better Together campaign members were sending each other text messages all through results night. 'Damn it, they've won Dundee...' *Bleep bleep* – my phone went off again: 'We've won Aberdeen!' I'd been up for 46 hours by then and I was told that I would appear on ITV's *Good Morning Britain* at 6 am to talk about the results. I felt sick from exhaustion. *Ring ring.* It was Ramsay Jones.

'Michelle, we've won with 55.3 per cent,' Ramsay announced.

'You beauty,' I screamed. Tears of joy and exhaustion streamed down my face.

'Go do *Good Morning Britain*. I love you – I can't thank you enough.'

Half of Scotland probably hate me now as a result of the campaign, but I don't regret any of it. Scotland, after all, was the winner: it was granted more power. I learnt so much – I learnt how to keep calm and I've become stronger and more confident. I think I took everyone by surprise and I took myself by surprise. This is how I want to be remembered by my kids – as the mum who went out there, despite all the threats, and was part of the team that saved the union – and I hope that one day they will be proud of their mum for being part of history.

I've faced and won battle after battle over the years but this is a victory I'll never forget.

EPILOGUE

My Fight to the Top

Rocky, starring Sylvester Stallone, was one of my favourite films when I was a kid. I was about ten or eleven, and I would dance around our tiny wee lounge in the East End to the theme song – 'Eye of the Tiger'.

Stallone's character – the boxer, Rocky – made me believe you only get somewhere in life if you work hard. I'm not kidding, that movie used to make me want to get out of bed in the mornings and fight. I thought I was Rocky; I would get up at the crack of dawn for my paper round and sing the 'Eye of the Tiger'. I used to run up and down the steps by the graveyard while I was delivering all the newspapers, imagining I was training for a boxing match.

So I literally couldn't believe it when one of the biggest motivational speakers in the USA asked if I'd like to come to one of their events in LA to tell my life story – alongside my childhood hero, as well as Al Pacino, in November 2014!

I'd never done a speech in the States before, let alone LA, the home of all the rich and famous – the home of Hollywood. Pop stars and actors always say that if you can crack America, then you've really made it. I saw it as a challenge – I was determined to leave a lasting impression.

I don't think the enormity of it all hit me until I arrived at LAX airport. A chauffeur-driven car picked me up to take me to my hotel. As I was driving down the famous Rodeo Drive in Beverly Hills, I saw my picture everywhere alongside Pacino and Stallone.

'Oh, my god,' I screamed, as I stared back down the street.

How could I go from growing up in the East End, to seeing my picture with some of Hollywood's biggest stars? It didn't seem real.

When I arrived at the Peninsular Hotel in Beverley Hills, a butler greeted me, and took me to my room. There were flowers everywhere, and champagne, and they had made a huge welcome display out of chocolates. They had even made a picture of me from cake icing.

Bloody hell! I thought as I fell back on the enormous bed.

I was so nervous as I arrived at the event the next day – I was absolutely shitting myself. I may have been known in the UK and Europe as one of the most in-demand female motivational speakers, but the Americans didn't have a clue who I was.

They are going to boo me off the stage, I thought. My hands started to tremble.

I was one of the first to speak, and the backstage crew were trying to clip a microphone onto my jacket, when that all too familiar feeling rose in my belly.

'I've got to go now,' I spluttered, running for the toilet.

I was sick in the toilet four times, that's how nervous I was. I kept running and coming back, running and coming back.

If that wasn't bad enough, I was about to be called on stage, when disaster struck. I still can't believe what happened next. All the pictures I use to help prompt me – pictures of the East End, pictures of the Launch of Ultimo – all 45 sheets of paper slipped out of my hands and scattered across the stairs.

Oh, my god. Why is this happening?

I never really use them, but they are reference points if I ever get stuck. If my mind was to ever draw a blank they were my safety net.

Someone was dashing around, desperately trying to pick them up while my name was being called out.

'Just leave it, leave it,' I told the woman. I'd run out of time.

I walked up on stage shaking like a leaf. There were 2,000 sets of eyes staring, and a spotlight beaming down on me. I felt like a rabbit caught in headlights. *What the hell am I going to do?*

So what did I do? I smiled. Just like every other time I'd felt out of my depth, whether that be my first dinner with Michael's parents, or speaking live on TV about the Referendum.

'Hi,' I said to the massive audience.

On the outside I was smiling, but on the inside, I was dying. The words were caught in my throat; my mouth was as dry as a desert.

And then something in me just suddenly snapped. The fighter in me burst out.

Michelle – why do you take these pictures with you everywhere, all around the world, but you never bloody look at them?

I always have this voice in my head telling me to fight harder.

It often speaks to me in the morning when I'm really tired, telling me to get my arse out of bed and get in the shower.

Michelle - get yourself together and get on with it.

I was having a conversation with myself in front of 2,000 people!

I took a deep breath; I focused on a few people in the front of the audience, and started to tell my story:

'I've always wanted to be in business, I wasn't the kind of teenager who had Madonna on my bedroom wall, I had a picture of Richard Branson above my bed,' I began.

'I decided to start up a business when I was ten-years-old. What I did have was passion, determination, and a can-do attitude, because if you've got those ingredients, then nothing will stop you,' I told the audience. I told them about the highs and the lows, how Ultimo nearly went bankrupt, and how we were saved in the eleventh hour. I revealed my struggles, just like I've told all of you reading this book.

Half an hour had passed. I was wrapping up, when the guy with the clipboard on the right of the stage signalled at me to keep going.

Oh Jesus. Deep breath.

I talked for an hour and 20 minutes in the end – that is the longest I've ever been on stage. I felt really nervous because no one had made a sound throughout the whole time I'd been up there. Normally the audience would be laughing, or clapping, but this lot had been so quiet you could have heard a pin drop.

'So thank you for taking your time to listen to my story,' I finished.

Silence. Oh Jesus this is embarrassing, I thought.

And then, I'm not kidding, the whole audience rose to their feet, clapping and cheering. They began cheering my name too, while hundreds of women came running up to the stage – it was really crazy, almost unreal.

I did it! What started out a disaster turned into one of the best speeches of my life. It was unreal, something like 1,000 people paid to have their picture taken with me. I swear I thought the queue would never end.

Looking back, I have to say that dropping those papers was the best thing that could have happened to me. I was so deep in the shit that I had to fight my way out of it. I always perform best when I'm in trouble, when I'm under the most amounts of stress and pressure.

Dropping those papers forced me to tell my story straight from the heart, to give an honest account of how I have got to where I am today – my fight to the top.

After the event, we all went to a restaurant to celebrate.

Back when I was growing up, mum and dad used to get so excited when a new film of Al Pacino's came out.

Bleep bleep.

It was a text message from my mum:

'You better come home with Al Pacino's autograph or I'm not watching your kids again,' she threatened. It made me laugh, as it was almost identical to what she had said when I'd had high tea with Prince Charles.

That was my cue – I approached Al Pacino.

'Al, my mum's at home watching my kids, could you sign this for her?' I smiled.

'Yeah, sure,' he said in his gravelly American voice. He was really friendly and down to earth for a Hollywood superstar.

I love Al Pacino's films, *The Godfather* and all the rest of them, but Stallone's *Rocky* was one of my all-time favourite movies. It was an inspiration for me, in terms of training and determination to win. I've never forgotten that movie. I was too embarrassed to say any of that when I met Stallone afterwards though.

'Hi,' I said, shyly. Stallone held out his hand and told me I had an incredible story. He was really smiley, but I was a bit surprised that I was taller than him!

Since the start of the year I'd been waking up every morning, thinking, I'd saved Ultimo, but is this the life I want now?

What next? I'm always thinking what's next. I just felt like I was missing something. I didn't want to be designing lingerie and swimwear for the rest of my life, I needed a new challenge.

'You know what Michelle, you only live on this earth once, it isn't a dress rehearsal. Do what makes you happy,' Mum said.

'If you feel like you need to do something to change your life then do it. You don't want to be sitting here in ten years time thinking you wish you'd done this or you'd done that,' she advised.

Mum was right. The kids were settled in our new place, the company had stabilised since my very public separation from Michael, I was starting to feel happier about being alone, and so I rang up my US business coach, Ted Anders.

'Ted, I'm lost,' I said. 'There is something still missing. Why could there be something wrong when I've won my company, my baby back?'

Ted came to my house in Glasgow and we locked ourselves in for two days, brainstorming. He helped me map out charts asking questions like: 'Who are you? Where do you want to go to next? What are you here for?'

'You're right, Ted, I'm here to try and make a difference.' I stood back and looked at the bigger picture. I decided I was going to put my heart into more speaking events, into mentoring those who need help.

I sold 80 per cent of Ultimo because I realised I didn't want to sit behind my desk for another five years designing lingerie and swimwear. I really care about Ultimo, and I still play a central role in the business for five days a month to guide the brand. But in terms of the day-to-day operations, I've hung up my bra. I've been offered many opportunities but I'm taking some time out to think about my next chapter. It's taken my fight to the top to realise that my real passion lies in inspiring people. My trials and tribulations have taught me how I can help others.

We all go through that dark place at some point in our lives – where we struggle to cope with things like: 'how am I going to pay for this? How am I going to get out of this?' We all go through it, but it's how we deal with it and stay strong that matters. I'm no expert, but through my life experiences I want to teach people how they can become the best they can be – whether that's in their career or in their lifestyle. I wouldn't have been sharing a stage with Al Pacino and Sylvester Stallone if I hadn't fought so hard for what I wanted.

As for Michael – he had his reasons for behaving the way he did, and I know that I'm not perfect. I wouldn't be the person I am today if none of it had happened. I'm at a stage of my life where all the bitterness has gone and all the fighting is over. He is now getting married to Sam, and I wish them all of the best, because I'm getting on with my life, and I'm about to start a new chapter.

I know I'll meet the perfect guy one day but I tell you what, I'm not going to wait around for it to happen. I'm too busy thinking, What next? Things don't come to you, you have to go out there and get them.

I'm back in the zone – I recently bought back 100 per cent of UTAN, a self-tanning range, and Ultimo Beauty from MAS Holdings and we're launching the brand into Boots and QVC. I've got a whole bunch of things I still want to achieve. I want to start new projects, tour around the world doing more speaking events and inspire people in fitness, diet, business and careers. I want to spend more time with my kids, spend more time with my family and spend more time working on 'me'. I want to get myself a life and, hopefully, one day fall in love.

Above all, I want my story to be inspirational. I want to show you that you can be a success, no matter where you came from.

I grew up in a culture where everyone said, 'You can't do this' or 'You can't do that' and I questioned it. Why does it matter where you are from? Why does it matter what education you managed to have? It doesn't mean your life is over if you don't have the best start. I'm living proof that there are no limits.

If I would have one bit of advice, it would be this: if you fail to plan, then plan to fail. I've always been a planner and I've always carried a book in my handbag listing what I have to achieve personally. I stay focused on that list. I try and tick every goal off. If I don't, that's okay. I'm not Superwoman, I have three children to look after and I take the list over to the next day.

So get yourself a notebook like mine, keep it in your bag and set yourself goals every day. Business goals and personal goals – and keep focused on those goals. Before you know it, it will be bedtime and you'll think – where did the day go?

If you're not successful, don't blame those around you. Don't blame him or her or *that* situation – blame yourself. You are in control of your life: if you have passion, an ambition or even the wildest of dreams, you can do it: just take control and never, ever give up. I hope this book will show it doesn't matter where you're from – whether you come from wealth or struggle to make ends meet – if you have the determination and a 'can-do' attitude you can achieve anything you want even if you've got to fight to get it. So do it – take control.

ACKNOWLEDGEMENTS

I would like to thank Mum and Dad for making me believe in my dreams and for bringing me up to respect everyone with manners; my three wonderful kids – Rebecca, Declan and Bethany – who have given me the determination to be a success; and my late Gran Philips for encouraging me everyday.

I would also like to thank my friends, including Bernard and Eileen Dunn and family; Nigel and Andrea Kelly; John Caudwell; Denise O'Leary; AP and Chanelle McCoy; Elena Ambrosiadou; John and Andrea Barnes; Peter and Teresa Løvenkrands, and to everyone else who has been by my side through everything – I can't fit everyone in but you know who you are!

Thanks too to my business associates Ted Anders, Sir Tom Hunter, Rob Templeman, Ian Grabiner, David Kaye, Mark Hollingshead, David Dinsmore, Claire Powell, Don McCarthy and all my speaking agents.

I would also like to thank Prince Charles and the Prince's Trust, the Ultimo Team, Deshamanya Mahesh Dayalal Amalean and the MAS Board.

Michelle Mone,
January 2015